MIRACLES
WHAT TO DO WHEN YOU NEED ONE

DR. DAVE MARTIN

Tulsa, OK

ENDORSEMENTS

Dave Martin has done it again! He has created a masterpiece to encourage your faith and create an expectation for miracles. In his new book, *Miracles: What to Do When You Need One*, he brings the Bible to life with modern-day stories that keep you excited and turning the pages. I believe the next page of *your* life includes miracles! This book creates an expectation that will help breed the miracle God has for you. I cannot encourage you enough to start making your miracle today by picking up this book and allowing it to help pave the road to your future.

David Crank
Senior Pastor of Faith Church
and author of *Solving Your Money Problems*

Dave Martin has been our dear friend for years, and this new book about miracles is tremendous. We needed a miracle when our daughter Lisa was born with the umbilical cord wrapped around her neck. Doctors said she might never walk or talk. But we got a miracle because my husband studied the Word of God and learned that Jesus has not changed, even if our denomination didn't preach it. Thank God, she is a mighty woman of God today.

Then in 1981, when I was diagnosed with liver cancer and given a few weeks to live, we saw had another miracle! We prayed at the foot of our bed, Jesus heard, had compassion and answered. That was 35 years ago! Remember Jesus loves you and He delights in answering your prayers. So study God's Word and it will be there when you need a miracle.

I salute you, Dave. This book will bless multitudes.

Dodie Osteen
Cofounder of Lakewood Church
Houston, Texas

In the introduction to his new book, *Miracles: What to Do When You Need One,* my longtime friend Dave Martin makes this profound statement: "If we could better understand the miraculous workings of God from His perspective instead of our own, we would probably see more displays of God's power in our lives." I say profound because these words are a powerful truth. Many people struggle with talking, understanding, and accepting miracles. While they accept that God may have performed the miraculous in the days of old, they reject the notion that the same is possible today. In this excellent piece of research, Dave manages, in very convincing fashion, to turn the tables on those naysayers—opening a vista of revelation that leaves even the most hardened of skeptics at a loss when it comes to disavowing the reality of miracles. Drawing attention to the world of God's miraculous power is what this book is about. It's about gaining a true knowing and understanding of what miracles are and, as Dave puts it, "how the miraculous intersects with the ordinary and how the supernatural overlaps the natural, what prompts God to do the impossible, and how miracles are actually realized in the believer's life." He validates that miracles, indeed, happen today. I believe in miracles, and I hope you do too. But even if you've been numbered among the skeptics, or have never witnessed a miracle, you owe it to yourself to read this book. Everyone will need a miracle at some point in life. This book will help you prepare to receive yours.

Henry Fernandez, Senior Pastor
The Faith Center
Sunrise, FL

From Genesis to Revelation the Bible is filled with examples of God making the impossible, possible. He was, is, and always will be, a God of miracles. In a generation hungry for an authentic experience of the supernatural power of God, it is imperative that we as Christ followers understand the power and purpose of the miraculous. Dr. Dave Martin's latest book is filled with biblical truth, Godly wisdom and practical examples. This book will encourage your faith and lift your expectation to see God do exceedingly and abundantly more than we could ever ask, think or imagine.

Andrew Kubala
Healing Evangelist
CEO Kubala Ministries International

I am so excited to see a book on miracles from my friend Dr. Dave Martin! There seem to be so many books explaining why miracles apparently don't happen that we seem to have turned the tide of Christianity towards nothing but psychological relief to endure the situations we are in. Miracles are all through the Bible and promised to all of God's people. We need an awakening to the next incredible season for the church; the miraculous flowing through every believer, in their everyday lives in a relevant, contemporary way.

Leon Fontaine
CEO of the Miracle Channel
Author of the *Spirit Contemporary Life*

Miracles are real, miracles are divine, and miracles change individual lives and global circumstances. In this insightful book, Dave Martin unlocks the topic of miracles and scripturally explains their purpose. He also shows us how to prepare for the miraculous because, at some point in our lives, we all will need a miracle. I encourage you to read this book, research the scripture, and be guided to your own miracle.

Terry Crist
Senior Pastor
Hillsong Phoenix

Contents

Why I Wrote This Book

I have spent my entire adult life in the ministry, devoting myself to serving the spiritual needs of others before I even graduated from college. Throughout the years in my work as a pastor, an international speaker, a published writer, and a success coach, I have found a need among people everywhere to experience the power of God in their lives.

It doesn't matter where people live. If they live in Australia, they will eventually need a miracle in their lives. If they live in Canada, they will need a miracle at some point. If they live in Europe or Africa or Asia or the United States, they will, from time to time, need to see the hand of God at work in their lives. And whether they are rich or poor, young or old, male or female, smart or just a pint short of a full gallon, there will be occasions that their needs cannot be met through normal channels and their problems cannot be solved through normal means. There will be times when only a miracle will do.

I was prompted to write this book since I encounter people in this situation almost on a daily basis. It doesn't matter where I roam. It doesn't matter who I meet. When I chat with other believers or rub shoulders with people who have never darkened the doors of a church, I find that the one common denominator between people of every age, nationality, background, and imaginable status in life is that they all eventually find themselves in circumstances that can challenge their security, threaten their dreams, endanger their relationships, or even jeopardize their physical lives. And deep down inside, they know there is little hope for them apart from the miraculous intervention of God.

Unfortunately, few people today have ever experienced a real miracle in their lives. Few people—and that includes believers—have ever even witnessed a real miracle. The question that haunts virtually every Christian is this: If the Bible is true, why don't we see the kinds of miracles in the world today that seemed to be commonplace for the people who lived when the Bible was being written? And if God is who He says He is and if He loves us the way He claims to love us, why don't we see in our lives the kind of miracles that marked the lives of Abraham, Moses, Elijah, and Paul?

I hate to see God's people struggling with matters of faith. I hate to see them struggling to rectify the things they read in Scripture with the things they experience in their lives. And I hate to see the doubt and confusion that results from a misunderstanding of God and the way that He works in the world, because, where there is an incomplete or erroneous interpretation of the Bible, disappointment is bound to follow. When people read one thing in the pages of Scripture and then experience something completely different in real life, they become confused. Then confusion is followed by doubt, and doubt leads to disbelief.

I have a passion to set the record straight. I have a consuming desire to help people everywhere understand what the Bible really says about miracles. The bottom line, of course, is that miracles are real and that God still performs them in this modern era. In fact, He may actually be performing more miracles today than at any time in human history. Yet, we do not realize this because the spiritual condition of the world continues to decline as the population continues to explode. And the church is pressing into uncharted territory at a rate never before witnessed in human history while the intensity of the resulting opposition is being increased.

People often fail to see miracles today—even when these people legitimately need one—because they do not understand the nature of miracles, the conditions under which God performs miracles, or the pathway that early believers walked in order to invite the miraculous intervention of God on their behalf. There are some definite and unchangeable "rules" in the Bible for the manifestation of God's miraculous power. Modern believers would do well to understand these "rules," because they reflect the thinking of God about the intersection of the natural world and the spiritual world.

If you are like most people, believers and unbelievers alike, you have probably faced a situation in your own life that prompted you to frantically cry out to God with the hope that He might do something unexpected to change your hopeless plight. Or perhaps you are facing a crisis like that right now. But if not, let me assure you that the day will come when you will need a miracle. Let me promise you that the day will come when you will need God to show His hand in your life. The day will come when you will need the Almighty to move heaven and earth on your behalf and to alter the circumstances that seemingly control your destiny. You will need Him to do something that is truly amazing, completely inexplicable, and totally captivating to those who are watching your life unfold.

I am writing this book so you can be prepared for your watershed moment tomorrow. I am writing this today so I can share with you both the principles from God's Word and the personal experiences from my own life that can help you better appreciate the "anatomy" of a miracle and how to apply God's laws of the miraculous to your earthly needs and battles.

God loves you, and He cares about you. He is not distant, as some would propose, and He is not detached from the details of your life. If something is important to you, it is important to Him. If something threatens you, it catches His attention. He is not silent, and He is not indifferent to the struggles you endure in this life, nor is He unaware of your weaknesses and vulnerabilities and your constant need for His help.

He "is able to do far more abundantly than all that we ask or think" (Ephesians 3:20, ESV). He is able to "astonish" us (see Mark 5:42) and to "amaze" us (see Mark 2:12). He is able to restore things in our lives that are destroyed, to change things in our lives that are improper, to heal things in our lives that are ailing, and to resurrect things in our lives that have died.

The Lord, however, must first find faith in our hearts before He acts. Faith is much more than just a mental adherence to the fact that God exists. It is much more than merely a presumption that God has the ability to do the things we imagine. Faith is rooted in the biblical teachings about God's miraculous power. It is grounded in an accurate understanding of what God expects from His people and what His people have a right to expect from Him.

So dig in and enjoy. Better yet, dig in and be changed. Grab your Bible and your note pad and find a comfortable place where you can open this book alongside the Book that tells us everything we need to know about God's perfect will. Then prepare to learn some things you probably didn't know. The answers to our legitimate questions are always in the pages of that wonderful Book. Somewhere in the Bible, God has addressed every concern that is relevant to our salvation and to the pursuit of His will for our lives. The answers to our questions about miracles are there, too.

Let your need for a miracle—whether past, present, or future—make you more open than ever before to the truths God wants you to grasp regarding His power and His willingness to manifest that power in your life and on your behalf. Let your curiosity about the miraculous nature of God make your heart more teachable than it has ever been, so God can help you understand what prompts Him to intervene in the lives of His people, and what motivates Him to change things that are seemingly unchangeable.

It is my desire to answer some of your questions about miracles throughout the pages of this book. You will also learn how miracles occur and what blueprint God typically follows as He manifests His power in the earth. But the primary purpose of this book is to incite your faith in God's willingness to get involved in your life, and help you tap into the infinite resources of the One whose glorious power can make the rest of your life—the best of your life!

Dr. Dave Martin

The View From Above: Miracles From God's Perspective

L et's start out by learning a new word. I don't really think of myself as an intellectual, nor do I think of myself as a theologian. But I do like to think of myself as a disciple (a learner under discipline). And for that reason, I do a lot of reading and a lot of research. I read my Bible regularly, and I constantly study other books that can help me grow as a person.

Since I do a lot of reading, I occasionally stumble across a new word that just seems to stick with me. The particular word I want to share with you is one of those types of words. It's the word *anthropocentric* (pronounced exactly the way it is written: anthro-po'-centric). I like this word because it says a lot and conveys an idea that I wish all Christians could grasp.

The word *anthropocentric* comes from two familiar Greek words. The Greek word *anthropos* means "man." We use this word every day. Anthropology is the study of mankind, and an anthropoid is something that resembles a human being in some way. The word *centric* is also Greek in its origins, and it means "in or at the center." We also use this word every day. Centric is just another word for "central," and a centrist is somebody who stands in the philosophical center of a political debate.

The word *anthropocentric*, therefore, is a compound word that simply means "man centered." A person who is anthropocentric is a person who tends to look at a particular issue from a human perspective or a human point of view. And that's where I want to begin this study of miracles.

I believe in God, and I believe in the Bible—every word of it! For that reason, I believe in miracles. Nobody could possibly read the Bible and fail to be impacted by the constant display of God's miraculous power, which seems to leap from every page of that ancient book. So the question for us in the twenty-first century is not whether God performs miracles; the question is whether God performs miracles today. And perhaps a secondary question is whether God would be willing to perform a miracle for each one of us specifically.

Personally, I believe that God does perform miracles today, and I believe that He is ready, when the situation demands it, to perform a miracle in my life or in the life of any believer who trusts in Him. Everybody needs a miracle at least once in his or her life. We need to understand how the miraculous intersects with the ordinary and how the supernatural overlaps the natural. We also need to understand what prompts God to do the "impossible" in this world, and how miracles are actually realized in the believer's life.

In order to understand this subject properly, we need to determine the perspective from which we want to view miracles. For instance, a football game looks quite different from the stands than it does from the Goodyear Blimp. In the same way, miracles look very different from God's perspective than they do from our perspective. It is my belief that if we could better understand the miraculous workings of

God from His perspective instead of our own, we would probably see more displays of God's power in our lives.

Unfortunately, however, too many Christians are anthropocentric in their approach to the things of God. They view everything from the human point of view. They view everything as if they are the center of the universe, and God is "out there" somewhere with the answers to all their needs. But if we want to fully understand God and His ways, we must come to the place where we start viewing our lives and the things that happen in our lives from God's point of view instead of ours. We must especially learn to view the supernatural from God's point of view.

Let me give you an example of what I'm talking about by asking you to take a look at the way you view the Christmas holiday season. When you were a child, how did you view Christmas? If you were like me, you got very excited as Christmas Day approached, because you knew you were going to receive about a thousand gifts and toys. You had some idea what Santa might leave for you under the tree (assuming that you believed in Santa Claus when you were a little kid). And you also had some idea what your mom and dad, your grandparents, and others might give you as gifts. But you weren't absolutely sure about those things, and you knew that you were bound to receive at least one or two gifts that would be totally unexpected. Christmas, to you back then, was a time of receiving and a time when you were the center of your family's universe.

When you became an adult, however, your perspective on Christmas changed. Especially if you are a parent, you became a "giver" instead of a "receiver." And while all parents know that it is a lot more gratifying to be a parent on the giving side of this equation than a child on the receiving side, no child ever considers what it must be like to be an adult at Christmastime. A child views everything about Christmas from his own limited point of view—a totally self-centered perspective.

A child knows absolutely nothing about his parents' experience of Christmas. The parents, on the other hand, know Christmas from both viewpoints: a child and a parent. And most of them, while holding fond memories of their childhood, would rather be the parent on Christmas morning than the child. They would rather see the excitement in their children's eyes than experience the delight of opening their own gifts.

Just like children on Christmas morning, we tend to view miracles solely from a self-centered perspective, a totally human perspective. We view miracles from the recipient's point of view instead of God's point of view, because we have never been in a position where we can perform a miracle for somebody else. But God *can* perform miracles. And for that reason, we need to understand what motivates Him to do the miraculous things He does.

Why does God perform miracles in some situations but not in other situations? Why does God respond quickly to one person's prayers while choosing to delay His response to another person's prayers? The answer to these questions are found in God's purposes for performing miracles. God is not an errand boy, and He is not Santa Claus. He is not sitting at His desk in His heavenly office, waiting for the phone to ring so He can quickly change into His Superman uniform and give us what we want. Yes, God loves us. And yes, God delights in giving good gifts to those who put their trust in Him (see Matthew 7:11). He cares about you and me, and He takes no delight in our suffering or deprivation.

God performs miracles for a bigger reason than those that drive us to pray. God acts in response to a more noble rationale than the one that inspires His children. We are compelled by our needs and our wants. We are motivated by our fears and our worries. When I need a miracle, I usually need to be rescued from circumstances I have created for myself or from a situation that others created for me. But God has a bigger goal in mind. He is concerned about the advancement of His kingdom and the glory of His Son. He is concerned about the realization of His purposes in the world and the fulfillment of His promises. Consequently, we would be much more inclined to see the miraculous power of God manifested in our lives if we would learn to pray from God's perspective rather than our own. We would be more inclined to witness demonstrations of divine power if we would trust God for the kinds of miracles that could directly contribute to His purposes in our lives.

I will have a lot more to say about this subject in the main text of this book, especially in chapter 3. I will also take more time in the chapters that follow to present a more complete theological argument for the point I am making here. But for now let me just offer you four reasons why God performed miracles for the men and women of the Bible, and why I believe He still performs miracles today. Let's look at the subject of miracles from God's point of view—and try to become theocentric (God-centered) in our thinking rather than anthropocentric (man-centered).

MIRACLES BRING GLORY TO GOD

When Jesus healed the paralytic who had been lowered by his friends through an opening in the roof of the house, Jesus told the paralytic to "pick up your mat, and go home" (Matthew 9:6, NLT). And when the man actually did what Jesus told him to do, the people "were filled with awe" (Matthew 9:8). So the miracle that Jesus performed that day created a sense of awe in the hearts of those who witnessed it. It brought honor to Jesus and to the Father He represented.

The Bible tells us that God is "jealous" when it comes to His name and His glory. In other words, He is very protective of His name and the glory that is rightly His. This is why the Third Commandment tells us that we should never use the Lord's name in a vain (empty, meaningless, careless) way. God disapproves of those things that dishonor His name, but He delights in those things that bring Him glory. He also delights in the people who bring Him glory, and He delights in those behaviors that bring Him honor.

God delights, therefore, in doing things that speak favorably of His name and that spread His name throughout the earth. And miracles achieve this purpose. Too many people and too many ideologies slander the name of the Lord. So, when circumstances warrant divine intervention, God takes pleasure in doing those things that cause people to view Him in a new and positive light and to think about their relationship with Him.

One of Jesus' primary motivations during those times when He performed miracles among the masses was to glorify the Father. This, too, should be one of the primary motivations in your life. To glorify God through your words, your deeds, and your attitudes is the height of practical worship. But you should also seek to glorify God when you pray. You should ask God miracles only when a miracle can highlight the loving nature of God and the awesome glory of the God you serve.

Whenever David prayed for deliverance from King Saul or whenever he prayed for divine protection in the face of death, he usually focused his prayers for a miracle on the end goal of glorifying God. "Then my soul will rejoice in the LORD," David told the Lord as he prayed for deliverance from his enemies (Psalm 35:9). "All the nations you have made will come and worship before you," David said to the Lord after he asked God to guard his life and deliver him from distress (Psalm 86:9).

So when you pray for God to heal an ailing family member or when you ask the Lord to provide an urgent need in your own life, remember God's glory, because God will be more inclined to respond positively to your cry for help if your motives flow from a grasp of the benefits He can derive by performing a miracle for you. After all, the eternal glory of His own name is more important to the Lord than the changing needs of your life or the life of any individual, because our troubles will eventually pass away and our problems will eventually be resolved. In time, we will forget about the troubles that loom over us today. But "your name, O LORD, endures forever" (Psalm 135:13, NLT).

MIRACLES STRENGTHEN THE FAITH OF BELIEVERS

Have you ever had a moment in your life when your faith became weak? All Christians have encountered difficulties in life that have challenged their faith or tested its depth. Peter's faith grew weak on occasion, and one man actually asked Jesus to "help my unbelief" (Mark 9:24, ESV). So it's not uncommon for believing people to experience moments of doubt and uncertainty. However, in those times, nothing can bolster one's faith quite like a miraculous demonstration of God's power.

Mary and Martha loved Jesus. They believed in Him as the promised Messiah, yet they also saw Jesus as a good friend and a trusted mentor. Therefore, when Jesus delayed the call of these two women to rush to Bethel to heal their dying brother, their faith was deflated by the Lord's delayed arrival three days after their brother's death.

We get a glimpse into the disappointment and the bitterness in Martha's heart through the words she said to Jesus when He finally arrived in Bethany, "Lord, if you had been here, my brother would not have died" (John 11:21). This statement shows us that Martha believed in Jesus as the all-powerful Son of God who was able to do supernatural things, but it also shows us that Martha's faith had been shaken and that she was feeling resentment toward the Lord because of His apparent unwillingness to respond to her urgent plea.

Martha's sister, Mary, also seemed equally shaken by the sudden death of her brother. But when Jesus stood before the entrance to the tomb and called to Lazarus to come out of that tomb, the faith of everyone who witnessed that astonishing event must have been elevated to celestial levels! And we know this to be true, because, before raising Lazarus, Jesus prayed to the Father, expressing His desire that the people watching this miracle unfold "may believe that you sent me" (John 11:42). Jesus wanted people to believe in Him as a result of the miracle He was about to perform.

Just think about this for a moment! Think about the way a genuine miracle can change the lives of those who witness it. On the night before Jesus' crucifixion, His eleven disciples went into hiding (Judas had already betrayed Him). The disciples were afraid of being arrested and fearful of being punished. They thought they might even be killed.

Days following the death of Jesus, His disciples hid behind closed doors and told lies in order to conceal their identities and obscure their association with the Nazarene.

But then something happened to change all that. The disciples were suddenly emboldened, and they became unafraid of death itself. In fact, historians tell us that ten of the eleven disciples of Christ died martyrs' deaths because they were more interested in preaching the Gospel than preserving their own lives.

So what changed for these eleven men? What happened that elevated their faith from the gutter to the mountaintop? They obviously had been changed by the resurrection of Christ. Jesus, Who had died on the cross, also foretold His own resurrection. And when the prediction of His resurrection came true, the miraculous nature of this event created so much faith in the hearts of these eleven men, nothing could restrain them any longer. Nothing could hinder their aggressive preaching and church-planting efforts. Nothing could make them afraid. The miracle of the resurrection created so much faith in their hearts, these men could never be the same again. They were even willing to die for the One who had risen from the dead.

So as you can see, God performs miracles to spread His good name throughout the earth, but He also performs miracles to build faith in the hearts of those who know him.

MIRACLES KNOCK DOWN BARRIERS TO MINISTRY AND CONFIRM THE GOSPEL OF JESUS CHRIST

I have a friend who used to work for one of the largest foreign missionary organizations in the world. He once told me about an event that took place shortly after he assumed his executive position in that organization as a young man in his mid-30s. This was a little more than a decade after the end of the war in Vietnam, and the leadership of this organization was negotiating with the Vietnamese government for the right to do some limited missionary work in that communist country.

One of the key players in these negotiations was a high-ranking Vietnamese official who was leading his government's investigation of the missionary association. He also was charged with the responsibility of either recommending or denying the organization's request. While the negotiations were taking place, the official's sister happened to travel from Hanoi to Paris to seek some urgent medical care for a serious illness. She had been diagnosed with cancer.

At that time Vietnam had a good relationship with the French government. In fact, the treaty that ended the war in Vietnam had been negotiated in France. The sister, therefore, of this high-ranking official felt quite comfortable in and around Paris.

While she was in France, the sister of the Vietnamese official decided to attend a Sunday service at one of the churches aligned with this missionary organization. During the service, she allowed the leaders of the church to pray for her. The top officials of the organization also began to pray for her. Soon afterward, the woman was miraculously healed. Of course, she told her brother. He was

aware of the prayers being offered on her behalf, and was so powerfully moved by this supernatural chain of events that he decided to
approve the organization's request and pave the way for this evange-
listic enterprise to start doing missionary work in his country. Consequently, the organization where my friend worked became the first
Christian organization in the United States to be allowed to openly
preach the Gospel in the communist country of Vietnam.

Miracles can suddenly open doors that are impossible for man
to open. Miracles can move mountains that men cannot move. Miracles can open minds and hearts that all the persuasion in the world
cannot influence. Miracles can leave doubters and naysayers with
absolutely nothing to say in response to God. In fact, the New Testament teaches that one of the primary purposes of miracles is to
confirm the message of God's Word and establish the lordship of
Christ. That is why the final verse in the Gospel of Mark tells us
that the disciples "went out and preached everywhere, and the Lord
worked through them, *confirming His word by the signs that accompanied it*" (Mark 16:20, Berean, emphasis mine).

I can't prove this objectively, but I personally believe that miracles are most prominent in churches that are pushing to enter new
territory with the Gospel. I believe that miracles are most common
in the lives of those individuals who are venturing into areas of obedience that they have never navigated before. History will validate
that when the church has been boldly aggressive in its approach
to world evangelization and when the church has been on offense
instead of defense in its efforts to proclaim the Good News, miracles
have always followed. But when the church has become complacent
and content with its gains and when the church has withdrawn to its
monasteries and its places of ease, the miracles have dried up.

It's just a fact: Miracles give credibility to the church's message,
while a lack of miracles gives rise to skepticism. According to the
Book of Acts, Philip was able to lead the way in taking the Gospel

across cultural boundaries into regions dominated by Gentile influences because "when the crowds heard Philip *and saw the signs he performed*, they all paid close attention to what he said" (Acts 8:6, emphasis mine).

People want to "see" the Gospel in all its power before they will be willing to "hear" the Gospel and respond to it. Philip wasn't the only preacher in the early church whose message was confirmed by displays of power. When Peter was traveling from Jerusalem to the Mediterranean coast, he stopped in the little city of Lydda to minister to the believers there. While in Lydda, Peter met a paralytic by the name of Aeneas, who was healed at Peter's command. Because of what God did for Aeneas through the command of Peter, "all those who lived in Lydda and Sharon saw him and turned to the Lord" (Acts 9:35). Then, on the same trip, in the port city of Joppa, Peter prayed for a woman named Tabitha, who had died. And when Tabitha was raised from the dead as a result of Peter's prayer, "it became known throughout Joppa, and many believed in the Lord" (Acts 9:42).

Virtually every chapter in the Book of Acts is packed with verses that tell us how the disciples healed ailing people, raised the dead, or proclaimed the wonders of God in languages they had never learned. And because of these miraculous occurrences and others like them, people were impacted. People were changed! People were saved!

But let's go back to a time before the events in the Book of Acts unfolded, to a time when the disciples were still trying to figure out who Jesus really was. At that time the disciples had been with Jesus for about two years, and they seemed to be grappling as individuals and as a group with the true identity of this man from Galilee. Could Jesus be the long-awaited Messiah, promised for generations by the prophets who preceded Him, or was He simply a great teacher and a mighty ambassador for God? In spite of Jesus' powerful teachings and in spite of the healings that accompanied His ministry, the disciples were still afraid to come out and publicly confess their beliefs about Him. But when they saw Jesus walking on the water in the midst of the storm and they saw him invite Peter to walk on the water with Him, they "worshiped Him, saying, 'Truly you are the Son of God'" (Matthew 14:33). Miracles annihilate doubt.

From your perspective and mine, miracles are a necessity. Often, they are the only means of escape from certain disasters in our lives. We are preprogrammed, therefore, to view miracles from the perspective of our own human needs. Miracles are God's prerogatives, which He can either grant to us in order to benefit our lives or withhold from us for a greater purpose that will become apparent some distant time in the future.

Rarely when we need a miracle do we contemplate what miracles mean to the Lord. To God the Father and to the Lord Jesus Christ, miracles are visible displays of divine power that are utilized to open closed doors, to authenticate a message that is often resisted by the world, to magnify and glorify the name of the Lord, and to strengthen the faith of believers while creating saving faith in the hearts of unbelievers.

Miracles are not actions that God takes simply to make life easier for those who invoke His name. Having said this, however, we must realize that there is an element of simple compassion that calls forth God's miraculous power.

MIRACLES HELP THOSE IN NEED

"The LORD is compassionate and gracious, show to anger, abounding in love," wrote David (Psalm 103:8). So God is not myopic, viewing people's lives solely from His heavenly perspective. God also understands the human plight from an earthly point of view. He "remembers that we are dust," so He understands our frailties and our utter need for His involvement in our lives (see Psalm 103:14).

Apart from God, the universe could not exist (see Colossians 1:17). And apart from God, you and I could not exist. We depend on God for the very air that we breathe, and we especially depend on Him for those things we cannot control. Unfortunately, most people do not accept this simple premise of life. They commit the most heinous of all sins when they assume that they are self-sufficient and capable of managing their own lives without the involvement of the Lord.

But those of us who know the Lord also know that we are incapable of wholly functioning apart from Him. We know that we are lost without His help, unable to see into the future and unable to manipulate the forces of life that steer us where we may not want to go. This is why God has compassion on people. Not only are people helpless (though they are too prideful to admit it); they also are ravaged by sin, which controls their thinking, their behavior, their destiny, and the quality of their lives. God is moved with compassion when we pray, and He is stirred to action when He sees us suffering needlessly.

When the two blind men outside Jericho cried out to Jesus to heal them, they simply said, "Have mercy on us" (Matthew 20:30). And in response, Jesus "had compassion on them and touched their eyes" (Matthew 20:34). Similarly, after Jesus had been teaching all day, He looked out over the crowd, and the Bible tells us that He saw the illnesses and the diseases of the people and that "he had compassion on them and healed their sick" (Matthew 14:14). So the Lord is "touched by the feeling of our infirmities" (Hebrews 4:15). He is moved by our legitimate human needs.

God cares when you have lost your job and you need income right away. He cares when your child is sick and you feel helpless to do anything about it. He cares when you are "sucker punched" by the betrayal of a friend, or even a spouse. He cares when you are rejected or lonely or emotionally wounded or afraid.

As you will discover in the opening chapter of this book, I embrace the broader definition of a miracle. While some people accept only the narrow interpretation of that word—defining a miracle as strictly a supernatural event that is objectively observable and that defies the physical laws of the universe—I believe that miracles can be smaller, subtler events. They can be personal events. To me, it is a miracle when God supplies much-needed money in an unexpected way. It is a miracle when God suddenly provides companionship for someone who has prayed for a friend for a long, long time. It is a miracle when God transposes a hard and bitter heart into a tender and teachable one. It is a miracle when a door opens in answer to prayer and there is no rational explanation as to how this event could have occurred.

I believe that God performs miracles—the big kind and the smaller kind too—because He has a greater and more eternal purpose in mind than we can imagine at the moment. I believe that God performs miracles because these inexplicable events can give credibility to the Gospel and draw attention to the Lord's glory. But I also believe that God performs miracles simply because He loves us and because He cares about our needs and our struggles. I believe that He performs miracles because He is moved in tremendous ways when He looks upon that isolated soul who dares to trust Him and dares to rely on Him and dares to expect with wholehearted anticipation the fulfillment of those promises that God has made to him through the written Word.

God works miracles because people believe in Him. It's that simple, yet that profound. He works miracles because it is His nature to change things that need to be changed. God has never been willing to accept the status quo that is the product of a faithless world. When God encounters genuine faith in the hearts of His people, He is inclined to change those things that they ask Him to change. And that, my friend, is the most basic definition of a miracle that I can offer. A miracle is simply a change in a person, a change in a situation, or a change in circumstances that only God can achieve and only God can explain. It is the elimination of what exists so that God can introduce what ought to be. And such wonders will always meet our needs, exceed our expectations, confirm God's Word, and glorify the name of the Lord.

CHAPTER 1

Name Your Miracle

Begin by focusing on that one thing you need from the Lord and get ready to witness a miracle in your life.

"In the beginning God created the heavens and the earth" (Genesis 1:1). You probably know this verse very well. It's the first verse of the first chapter of the first book in the Bible. You can quote it without even trying. And you know what follows: The six days of creation.

But have you ever considered all the wisdom and knowledge that are contained in this little verse? For one thing, this verse gives us the Bible's first revelation of the nature of God. We learn from this little verse that God is more than one person (the Trinity). How can we discover that God is more than one person from this little verse? Because the word for *God* in this verse is a plural word that actually means "Gods!"

Another thing we find in this verse is the origin of the three basic components of the universe. The universe consists of matter (the physical elements), space, and time. There is nothing else in the universe. These are the three components that comprise everything we know in the physical realm. But in this little verse, we see the origin of all three of these components: God created the heavens (the Hebrew word here means "open space"). God created the earth (this Hebrew word refers to the "elements" or "matter," not the planet Earth). And God created time ("in the beginning"). So this tiny little verse shows us the origin of everything we know and everything we accept as real.

Another interesting thing that strikes us in this verse is the verb *created*. The verbs in the opening chapters of Genesis tell us a lot about God. The things He did can give us a glimpse into His nature. Among other things, we know that God "said," He "saw," He "separated," He "set," He "blessed," and He "gave." But the first thing that God ever did was to "create." He created matter, space, and time.

The word *create* is an interesting word in itself. Look carefully into the biblical account of the six days of creation and you will notice that God created only three things. God created the heavens and the earth on the first day of creation (see Genesis 1:1), He created physical life on the fifth day of creation (see Genesis 1:21), and He created man on the sixth day of creation (see Genesis 1:27). Everything else, God "made." He "made" the sky (see Genesis 1:7). He "made" the sun, moon, and stars (see Genesis 1:16). And He "made" the animals that inhabit the land (see Genesis 1:25).

To "make" something is to craft a new thing out of material that already exists, but to "create" something is to call into existence that which has no material existence. Surprisingly, God only created three things: the physical universe (matter, space, and time), life, and man. Then God "made" everything else out of these three components.

Like God, you and I, who are formed in His likeness, have the power to "make" things. He granted us this ability. He granted us the ability to take existing materials and existing sounds and to "make" new things out of those materials and sounds. He made us so we could "rearrange" the things that already existed in His universe in order to form new things that would be useful for our purposes. But only God can "create" something. Only God can call into existence that which had no existence before He imagined it and created it.

God "created" the physical elements out of nothing, a feat that man will never duplicate. God "created" physical life when there was no physical life, another feat that man will never duplicate. And God "created" man, a physical creature who required a unique act of creation, because he was not merely another type of animal (as evolutionists would have us believe). Man was uniquely "created" in the likeness and the image of God to have a moral character, a conscience, the ability to distinguish right and wrong, the ability to ponder his own origins and purpose, and the ability to make his own choices and to plot the course of his own life.

These things in the book of Genesis fascinate me, and I wish I could take the time to expound on them here. In Genesis, every little word and every little phrase seems to possess the most profound significance. And when rightly understood, these ancient revelations of God reveal to us incredible things about God's nature and God's way of thinking.

Since this book is about miracles, I will avoid the temptation to bloviate about other topics, and I will focus on the subject at hand. I will write about those things that pertain to the miraculous acts of God. And with this focus in mind, I want to go back to the opening verse of the Bible, because in this little verse we also find the very first revelation in God's Word pertaining to the nature of the miraculous.

You see, when God "created" the heavens and the earth, He simultaneously created two overlapping realities. Before this initial act of creation, nothing existed except God Himself. That's hard to imagine. That is difficult to grasp with the finite human mind.

Think about it—before there was physical matter, there was nothing, not even a particle of dust. Before there was empty space, there was nothing, not even empty space (that's hard to imagine). And before there was time, there was no such thing as a minute or an hour (also hard to imagine). But then God spoke, and instantaneously there was empty space filled with all the physical elements that comprise our universe. And time as we know it began.

Notice that God created two spheres at the same time that were designed to coexist side by side. He created the earth (the material elements that constitute our tangible world and the rest of the universe), and He created the heavens (a plural word, which describes the empty space we know as "sky," the vast resources of "outer space," and the invisible realm we know as "Heaven"). He created the physical world and the spiritual world simultaneously. And since that very first day, both of these worlds have existed in harmony as God's two spheres of operation. God created both the "heavens" and the "earth." He created both the spiritual world and the physical world—the natural and the supernatural—and He pronounced both of them to be "very good" (Genesis 1:31).

Since that first day of creation, both the spiritual world and the physical world have been impacted by the introduction of sin (Satan's rebellion in Heaven and man's rebellion on Earth). Nevertheless, God is still the God of both Heaven and Earth. He is the creator of both realms, and He is the sustainer of both realms. But because He is the designer and architect of both worlds, many of the same principles apply in both worlds.

For instance, you will find the law (or principle) of the harvest in both worlds. What does this mean? This means that, in both worlds, you reap what you sow (see Galatians 6:7). In the physical world, if a man sows corn, he will reap corn. If he sows soybeans, he will reap soybeans. Likewise, in the physical world, a man will reap what he sows.

The same principle applies in the spiritual world, as well. In the spiritual world, "whoever sows wickedness reaps trouble" (Proverbs 22:8, ISV). And "the one who sows to please his flesh, from the flesh will reap destruction" (Galatians 6:8, Berean) while "the one who sows to the Spirit will from the Spirit reap eternal life" (Galatians 6:8, ESV).

In both the physical realm and the spiritual realm, you reap *what* you sow. But in both realms, you also reap *more than* you sow. For instance, if a man plants one kernel of corn in the physical ground, he will reap hundreds of kernels of corn at harvest time. If a man forgives others who trespass against him (a small thing), God will forgive that man for his own trespasses (a big thing).

So as you can see, in both worlds, you reap *what* you sow and you reap *more than* you sow. But in both worlds, you also reap *after* you sow. No matter how much you want to hurry things along, you can't eat the corn until you plant the corn and wait for the corn to grow. And no matter how much you want to realize God's promises in your life right now, you can't reap the benefits of God's promises until you obey all the commands that are attached to that promise and then wait for the Lord to act. In God's perfect time, the blessings will flow, but God's blessings always follow man's obedience. This is the law of God in both the physical realm and the spiritual realm. This is the law of the harvest.

In fact, there are so many similarities between the physical world and the spiritual world that Jesus was able to use the physical world every day of His life to help His followers understand the unseen things of the spiritual world. Jesus knew Heaven quite well, but His followers had never been to Heaven. So Jesus looked at the natural world to find things that were familiar to His disciples so He could use those familiar things to help His disciples understand the eternal spiritual concepts He was trying to convey to them.

For example, He used lightning to help them understand prophecy (see Matthew 24:27). He used children to help them understand humility (see Matthew 18:3). He used mustard seeds to help them understand faith (see Matthew 17:20). He used pearls to help them understand the superiority of eternal life over earthly life (see Matthew 13:46). And the list goes on.

Jesus was easily able to reach into the familiarity of the physical world and utilize all kinds of natural things to help His disciples understand the spiritual world they had never seen. And Jesus could do this because a lot of things are the same in both worlds. A lot of things are the same in Heaven and on Earth, because the same mastermind created both worlds and the same architect drew up the plans for both worlds. Heaven will be more familiar to you than you might think.

As humans, we tend to make the relationship between Heaven and Earth more complicated than it ought to be. We think of Heaven as misty and magical and mysterious and strange. We tend to think of it as lacking physical substance. In fact, we can't fully explain *what* we visualize in our minds when we think of Heaven. We think of Earth as being hard and cold and lacking any spiritual relevance. It is something that will be used up and thrown away, because we think that God doesn't really like material things. We think that He prefers spiritual things. But nothing could be further from the truth. In Heaven, we will have physical bodies and walk upon the physical ground. On Earth, God wants us to "live in the Spirit" and "walk in the Spirit" (Galatians 5:25, KJV). In God's mind, the two kingdoms aren't that much different and they aren't that far apart, even though they are temporarily divided by the persistent problem of human sin.

Miracles, therefore, aren't what we sometimes imagine them to be. Miracles aren't these impossible, improbable, and unpredictable acts of God that defy all logic from an earthly perspective. Although they can involve a temporary suspension by God of the physical laws of the universe, they do not defy the original relationship that God established between the physical world and the spiritual world. In fact, miracles are those acts of God that cause these two worlds to overlap for a moment in time.

What is a miracle? According to the *New Oxford American Dictionary*, a miracle is "a surprising and welcome event that is not explicable by natural or scientific laws and is therefore considered to be the work of a divine agency." But even the *New Oxford American Dictionary* recognizes that the word *miracle* can mean different things to different people. For this reason, the dictionary further defines a miracle as "a highly improbable or extraordinary event, development, or accomplishment that brings very welcome consequences."

So that which represents a miracle to you may not be a miracle to someone else, while someone else's miracle may not be a miracle to you. Nevertheless, the fact remains that a miracle is a miracle. If you need something from the hand of God that you cannot produce by your own efforts, you will recognize God's intervention in your life as a miracle, no matter how others may characterize that event.

For the purposes of this book, I want to adopt the same two definitions of a miracle that the *New Oxford American Dictionary* offers us. On the one hand, a miracle is the temporary suspension of the physical laws that God wove into the fabric of his creation. These kinds of miracles are powerful. They also defy human logic, and they occur infrequently.

In the Bible, we see many of these kinds of miracles, but you have to take into account the fact that the Bible covers at least 4,000 years of human history. So even though there are lots of examples of these profound, logic-defying acts of God within the pages of Scripture, these occurrences were spread out over many centuries. They were not everyday events. When necessary, however, God did not hesitate to stop the rotation of the Earth (see Joshua 10:12–14), to reverse the rotation of the Earth (see 2 Kings 20:8–11), to raise the dead (see John 11:38–44), or to cause the sea or other bodies of water to part so his people could walk through the water on dry ground (see Exodus 14:15–22; Joshua 3:14–17).

These are the kinds of miracles that don't happen every day, and they shouldn't happen every day. If they did happen regularly, human beings could not conduct their daily lives. There are approximately 7 billion people on this planet, and these people count on the sun rising every morning. They count on gravity operating when they go to bed at night. They count on water freezing at 32 degrees Fahrenheit (0 degrees Celsius). And they count on snowstorms in the winter and rainstorms in the summer. A disruption of these kinds of natural laws would constitute a miracle. But just imagine what kind of world this would be if the suspension of these natural laws occurred every time somebody requested it. Life would come to a grinding halt.

So God doesn't cause iron to float very often, but he did cause iron to float when it served his purposes in a particular situation (see 2 Kings 6:1–7). And God doesn't usually allow donkeys to talk, but he did allow a donkey to talk when it served his purposes (see Numbers 22:28). The first kind of miracle that we find in the Bible, therefore, is the type of dramatic miracle where God temporarily suspends one of the fixed laws of the physical universe in order to accomplish a specific divine purpose that could not be accomplished through ordinary means. God has performed these kinds of miracles throughout human history, and he will perform them again. The Bible tells us so. But God does not perform these kinds of miracles often, and he does not perform them simply for the convenience of his people or to impress doubters or bolster the faith of his followers.

The kind of miracle that God does delight to perform for his people is the second kind of miracle, the kind that is "a highly improbable or extraordinary event, development, or accomplishment that brings very welcome consequences." And usually, this is the kind of miracle that God's people pray for God to provide: a supernatural intervention of God in the problems of an individual human life.

But when we think of miracles in these simpler terms, it becomes obvious that all of us need miracles from time to time. I need miracles in my life; you need miracles in your life. In fact, there is something that every believer wants God to do in his or her life right now. So what do you need from the Lord at this moment in your life? Do you need his supernatural help with a particular problem that is troubling you? Do you need him to do something improbable and extraordinary in your life that you cannot do for yourself? Then you need a miracle.

Always be aware that there are some things you need from God that cannot come through a miracle. There are some things that can only come through obedient living or hard work. If you want to know more about God's Word, for instance, you need to study God's Word (see 2 Timothy 2:15). God is not going to fill your head with biblical knowledge while you are watching television. And if you want to lose weight, you need to increase your physical activity and stop eating so much junk food. God is not going to knock 50 pounds off your flabby thighs while you are soaking in the hot tub.

But God is delighted to do those things for you that you cannot do for yourself. He is delighted to go where you cannot go, to say what you cannot say, to be what you cannot be, and to do what you cannot do. If you are faithful with the things in life that you *can* do, God will be pleased to do those things that you *cannot* do. And if you are obedient with the part of the equation that God has placed in your hands, he will be faithful with the part of the equation that you can't handle. And that's the anatomy of a miracle.

In a moment of time, God can change a life. He can change a heart. He can change a person's attitude or a person's destiny. In a moment of time, God can change a situation. He can call forth resources that did not exist when you got out of bed this morning, and he can erase problems that exhaust your strength or deplete your joy. In a moment of time, God can change a relationship. He can heal a marriage, restore a father to his son, repair a broken heart, or send forth a spirit of forgiveness to help two lifelong friends mend their relationship.

God delights in doing the impossible and the improbable. In fact, that is his primary business. He delights in taking that which is dead and causing it to live again. He delights in taking that which is hopeless and causing it to thrive. He delights in taking that which is broken and restoring it so it is better than it was before. He delights in taking the tail and making it the head, in finding a person who is on the bottom and lifting that person to the top (see Deuteronomy 28:12–14).

If we didn't need the impossible and the improbable, we wouldn't need God, because God's name is synonymous with the world of the supernatural. And every miraculous thing God has ever done since the day he created the heavens and the earth is something that defies human expectation and human rationale. God just loves to do those things that unbelieving people have no way to explain.

So as we prepare to engage the subject of miracles, I want to encourage you to open your mind and your heart. When you finish this book, I think you will see that miracles are not what you thought they were. Miracles are not these fabricated occurrences of chance that people claim they have received from God, yet which make no sense and which serve no good purpose. Miracles are not the inventions of overly emotional and easily misled fools who are gullible enough to believe in fairy tales.

Miracles are real. They happen all the time. They happen all around us. And they *can* be validated. But apart from God, they cannot be explained. The only rationale behind these unexpected and inexplicable events is the direct intervention of the creator of Heaven and Earth, who alone has the power to reach out of the unseen realm of the spiritual world in order to achieve his purposes in the very visible realm of the physical world.

When you finish this book, I think you will also come to realize that God has done a lot more miraculous things in your life than you might imagine. And he wants to do more. So to help you understand miracles and to help you understand how they can operate in your life, I want you to focus right now on that one thing you need from God more than anything else. I'm not talking about something you can do for yourself. I'm not talking about something that can be obtained through your own efforts. I'm talking about something that you need from the hand of God that cannot possibly come from any other source. Something that is completely impossible or improbable without the direct intervention of the Lord!

Whatever that thing may be in your life, I want you to hold onto it and use it as your focal point while we proceed through this study of miracles, because this book will explain to you the eight biblical principles for unlocking the miraculous power of God in your life. These "keys" will definitely work for you if you have a legitimate need that requires the intervention of God. They have worked in my life and Christine's life, and they have worked in the lives of countless other believers I know. Whatever the need may be in your life right now, you can expect a miracle from the Lord if you will embrace the concepts presented in the following pages and put them into practice in your life.

But the first thing you need to do is know what you need from the Lord. God responds to specific prayers, and he responds to specific needs. It's not a bad thing to pray, "Lord, bless me." But that kind of prayer is so general, so vague, you can't really tell whether God has answered it or whether the answer is still on the way. The kind of prayer you need to pray if you want to see a miracle in your life is something like, "Lord, bless me this coming year by increasing my income $1,000 a month." Now that's the kind of prayer that

God can wrap himself around, and that's the kind of prayer that, when answered, will build your faith to levels you have never known, because it is specific and it requires a measurable response. It is not vague. You will know when God answers it.

A ship never picks up anchor and sets sail until the captain of that ship has a destination clearly in mind, and an airliner never leaves the runway until the pilot has a destination clearly in mind. You, too, need a destination, a goal, if you want to see a miracle in your life. You need to set something specific before the Lord and present that need to him if you want to receive the answer you seek. But unfortunately, too many Christians are vague with their faith, so they don't even recognize a miracle when God sends one their way.

One Sunday evening, a lady came up to me after a church service and wanted me to pray for her. Her mortgage and a couple of other bills were due and she didn't have the money to pay them. When I asked her what she wanted me to pray about, she said, "I need more money."

So I said, "How much money do you need?"

She said, "More. I just need more money."

So I said, "How much more?"

She said, "I don't know. I just know that I don't have enough. I've got bills I can't pay, so I need God to provide me with more money."

I wasn't really sure how to pray for this woman. She had a legitimate need, but she didn't know precisely *what* she needed. Several years ago, when Christine and I were trying to get out of debt, I could tell you to the penny how much money I needed in order to pay off all our debts. I kept a running total on the refrigerator door that I updated every day so I would know exactly how much money I needed in order to be debt-free. But this woman had no idea how much money she needed. She just wanted "more." If I had wanted to be harsh with her, I could have handed her a dollar bill, and that would have satisfied her prayer request for "more money." But instead of being harsh, I took the time to try to teach her an important biblical principle: If you want God to do something specific in your life, you need to be specific with your faith.

Marilyn Hickey once spoke with a friend of mine who was trusting God to give him a wife. So Marilyn asked the man if he had ever made a list of all the specific qualities he wanted in a wife. "No," he said, "I've never made a list like that."

So Marilyn Hickey encouraged him to go back to his hotel room and spend some time making a list of all the specific traits he wanted in a wife. The next morning, he returned to the conference and started talking again with Marilyn, who asked him if he had drawn up his list.

"I did," he said, and he pulled out the four-page list to present to her.

"My goodness," she said, "four pages. That's quite a list. Did you show it to God?"

"I did," he replied. "And what did God say?" she inquired.

"God said if he could find a woman like that, he'd probably get married himself," my friend said jokingly. But the point here is that we need to be specific with the Lord.

Toward the end of his earthly ministry, Jesus traveled through the city of Jericho on his way to Jerusalem. But as Jesus was leaving Jericho, two blind men, who were sitting by the roadside, shouted to him, "Lord, Son of David, have mercy on us" (Matthew 20:30). And because they continued to shout at Jesus when he appeared to ignore their cries (more about this in chapter 3), Jesus finally responded to the two blind men. But Jesus' response probably seemed strange to those around him. He called to the two men, asking them, "What do you want me to do for you?" (Matthew 20:32).

Are you kidding me? What kind of question was that? They were blind! They were sitting on the side of the road, calling at the top of their lungs for help, because they could not see anything. Anybody standing there would have known what these two blind men wanted from Jesus. These two men wanted to be healed. They wanted to see. And the omniscient Son of God should have known what these two men needed from him.

But Jesus wanted to hear them say it out loud. He wanted to hear them define their need specifically and put their request into words. He wanted to know the exact miracle they were asking God to perform in their lives. Before he would do anything to minister to their need, Jesus wanted to know the particular act that would address their greatest need and demonstrate to them God's love and God's power. So before he called forth the miraculous power of God, Jesus first required that these two men tell him precisely what they wanted him to do.

Like a ship at a loading dock or an airplane at a passenger terminal, you cannot leave where you are until you decide exactly where you would rather be. So the first thing you need to do if you want to see a miracle in your life is to decide where you would rather be. What is it that you want God to change? What is it that you want him to provide? What is it that you want him to remove or heal or resurrect? What is it that you want him to do for you that you cannot do for yourself? What is it?

Begin by getting specific with God. Begin by choosing just one thing—something that is vitally important to you and something that could never possibly occur apart from the direct intervention of God—and put that thing into words. Name it, then write it down and focus on it. And use that thing as your focal point while we work our way through this book and through the remaining seven principles for activating the miraculous power of God in your life. If you will get specific with your need, God will get specific with his answer. And you will see the mighty hand of God in your life.

CHAPTER 2

Confirm Your Miracle

Find the biblical teaching or biblical precedent that confirms God's willingness to provide the miracle that you seek.

Have you ever heard a Christian pray, "Father, if it be thy will"? Have *you* ever prayed, "Father, if it be thy will"? Christians pray "if" prayers all the time. "*If* it be thy will, please heal me." "*If* it be thy will, please provide for me." "*If* it be thy will, please save my unbelieving husband." But I don't believe in most "if" prayers. In fact, I think these kinds of prayers are more accurately described when we call them what they really are: "sissy" prayers.

Now before you get angry with me, just know that I've prayed a few "sissy" prayers myself. But one day I finally realized that there aren't a lot of "if" prayers in the Bible. In the Bible, God answered the specific prayers of people who dared to name the exact things they wanted God to do for them. These great men and women of faith didn't hide behind the word *if.* They didn't give God or themselves a way out of the prayer. They just put their requests out there and waited for God to say "yes" or "no." There was no room for compromise.

I believe "if" prayers have become popular today for two reasons. First, a lot of people don't really know what they need from God or what they want God to do for them. They believe they want a better paying position at work, and they think they need more income. But they aren't really sure how much additional income they actually need, and they aren't really sure if they should be asking for a new position at their current place of employment or a completely new job somewhere else. This causes them to hide their uncertainty and doubt by wrapping their misgivings in that little word "if."

The second reason people pray such wimpy prayers is because they don't really believe that God can answer their prayers. They want to provide God with an excuse for not responding to their specific pleas. In case God doesn't come through for them, they want to be able to defend God's reputation and protect His name from the many doubters who are looking for a reason to mock Him. They want to be able to defend the faith that they claim to hold by making sure they are always in a position to say, "Well, it must not have been God's will."

But I believe God wants us to be specific with our prayers. God responds to faith—not doubt. He responds to people who get out of the boat and start walking on the water, not people who dip their toes in the water first to see if it's safe and to see if the temperature is suitable for them.

On the other hand, the overly "cocky" prayer can be just as damaging to the name of Christ as the impotent "sissy" prayer, if we don't know how to pray according to God's will. While the spiritual weakling seeks to protect God's name and his own reputation by creating a built-in escape hatch for his failed prayers, the person with a warped understanding of faith often reaches beyond the realm of sanity with his misguided prayers. The weakling prays, "If it be thy will," while the cocky spiritual showman prays openly for things that God will never grant to him because those things aren't based on any biblical teaching and won't achieve God's purposes in that person's life.

The people of God must learn to pray rightly. We must learn to pray the prayers that God wants us to pray. God desires to hear our prayers and He desires to answer our prayers, but He will only answer those prayers that reflect His will for our lives. Therefore, before we pray, we must know *what* to pray. And in order to know *what* to pray, we must study the Scriptures.

Just think about it! When Moses lifted his staff high above his head and extended it toward the sea that stood before him, he knew precisely what he wanted God to do for him. When he lifted his voice and boldly commanded the people to "stand still, and see the salvation of the LORD" (Exodus 14:13, KJV), he knew precisely what God wanted to do through him. There was no uncertainty with Moses, and there was no uncertainty with any of the great men and women of faith we find in the Bible. When these men and women prayed, they prayed with specific focus and they prayed with specific language that defined their specific needs with specificity. (Get the point?) Then when they commanded God's will to be executed, they spoke to the rocks and to the clouds and to the water and to the lifeless bodies of people who had died with words of authority, certainty, confidence, and conviction. There were no "if" prayers in any of these situations, and there were no "if" commands to the elements or the circumstances that these people faced.

Now one of the few situations in the Bible where someone prayed, "If it be thy will" was the time when Jesus was praying in the Garden of Gethsemane, asking the Father to remove the cup of suffering that He would have to partake the next morning (the crucifixion). But Jesus could rightly pray this prayer at that time because He knew what God actually wanted Him to do. He knew the perfect will of God in the matter of His approaching death. Jesus wasn't seeking to discover the will of God. The problem Jesus was facing was that He knew the will of God all too well, so He was trying to avoid it by changing God's mind.

Jesus was crying out to God, not in an effort to determine God's will in the matter of His pending crucifixion, but in an effort to change God's mind about the matter (more about changing God's mind in the next chapter). Jesus clearly knew the will of God regarding the events that were about to unfold in Jerusalem, so Jesus wasn't praying an "if" prayer to cover His lack of faith or lack of understanding. Instead, Jesus was asking the Father to consider changing His approach. He was asking the Father that, "if" it was possible, He would like the Father to "let this cup of suffering be taken away from me" (Matthew 26:39, NLT).

If you want to pray with power, you need to know what God wants so you can focus your prayers on that specific issue. And if you want to see miracles in your life in response to your specific prayers, you need to know the difference between spiritual fantasy and the miracles that God will actually perform for you. However, the only place you can go to learn how God thinks about such things is the Bible. In the Bible, God reveals to us how He thinks and how He acts in response to our faith and our prayers.

It is always a good thing to begin your journey toward a miracle by naming the miracle your heart desires. The heart is the best place to discover the will of God, because God speaks to us primarily through our hearts, not our minds. Nevertheless, the heart can be deceitful (see Jeremiah 17:9). Although God speaks to His people through their hearts and leads them through their hearts, the heart can lie like a rug. It can make us believe things that are not true. It can mislead, misdirect, and cause otherwise sane individuals to chase phantoms and to put their trust in fairy tales that have no basis in reality. For this reason, every great spiritual pursuit must begin in the deep recesses of the human heart, but it must conclude by lining up with the objective realities of God's Word. God leads us through our hearts, but he makes His will known to us through His written Word. So when both the heart and the Scriptures align, the believer can move forward in confidence with both his head and his heart supporting him.

There's an interesting little verse in the book of Acts that describes an unusual approach to the things of God by some people living in the small Macedonian community of Berea. In the first century A.D., the apostle Paul traveled to Berea with Silas to preach the Gospel there (see Acts 17:10–15). As they did elsewhere in the Mediterranean world, Paul and Silas began their ministry in Berea by entering the synagogue and proclaiming the resurrection of Jesus to the Jews and the Gentile converts to Judaism. And the Berean Jews were unusually receptive to Paul's message. They received the Word of God "with great eagerness" (Acts 17:11).

But their eagerness (a heart condition) was tempered by their insistence on examining "the Scriptures every day to see if what Paul said was true" (a head condition). The preaching of Paul stirred their hearts. But by searching the Scriptures to verify Paul's teachings, the Bereans satisfied their minds, as well. And this is the way God wants all His people to respond to Him. In fact, God described the Berean people as having "more noble character" than some of the other believers in the Mediterranean world, because the Bereans believed God, but they believed Him without falling into the subtle trap of relying solely on the tug of their hearts while rejecting the logical needs of their minds.

Years ago, I heard a funny story that really drives home this point. This story is not based on any trustworthy theology, but it still makes a good point.

It seems that there was a new soul in heaven who was soon going to be born as a baby on earth. So God assigned this new soul to an angel, who introduced himself to the new soul and told the new soul that it was time for him to visit Heaven's warehouse so he could pick out all the physical traits he would be utilizing during his earthly life. The angel gave the new soul $777 from the Bank of Heaven and escorted him to the warehouse.

"What's the money for?" the new soul asked.

"That's the money you will need to buy the physical traits you want most in your earthly body. We have a 'standard' version of every physical trait, and the 'standard' version is always inexpensive. But if you want any physical attributes that are exceptional, you will have to pay for them. And you only have $777, so you need to spend it wisely."

Then, with that important information in hand, the new soul followed the angel into the Hair Department, where the new soul had the option of buying any type of hair he wanted. Of course, the best heads of hair were more expensive than the stringy hair or the thinning hair, so the new soul decided not to spend all his money on hair. He knew he would want to spend most of his money on other things.

And with this philosophy guiding him, the new soul followed the angel around the warehouse to all the different "departments," purchasing all the different physical features that would be part of the earthly body. He bought his hair, his eyes, his height, his weight, his hands, his feet, his muscle mass, and everything else he would need for the body he would use on Earth.

Then finally, with $175 remaining in his pocket, the new soul followed the angel into the Brain Department, and the new soul walked around slowly, studying all the different brains that were available for purchase. The brains were labeled with their various characteristics and their various prices, but the new soul noticed one brain in particular that was really quite expensive. The sign beneath this brain said, "Christian Brain," and the price tag was $695.

"Wow, that brain costs a lot of money," the new soul said. "I would have to return just about everything I've bought so far just to be able to afford that brain. Why is that brain so cotton pickin' expensive?" he asked.

"Oh, that's our Christian brain," the angel told the new soul. "It's our highest priced model because it's never been used."

Fortunately, the Bereans weren't like a lot of modern Christians. The Bereans actually used their brains. They actually listened to the "still, small voice" that was resonating in their hearts, and compared that powerfully persuasive voice to the Word of God before they would allow themselves to yield to it. They accepted nothing at face value, and they did not trust their own hearts. Instead, they examined every word they heard in order to test the accuracy of the message.

We, too, should take everything that is impacting us and compare it with the Word of God to test its spiritual authenticity. God's high praise for the Bereans leads us to understand that the Lord is never offended when we test those things that are influencing us spiritually. He is never offended when we move cautiously in response to the spiritual urgings that are tugging at our hearts.

If God wants to lead you into a new spiritual experience or to stretch your faith or build your character, He will always begin by speaking directly to your heart. But then He expects you to compare what your heart is telling you with the objective truths of the Bible to confirm that you are indeed hearing God's voice rather than a counterfeit "voice" that has arisen from your own subconscious desires or the subtle influences of the people around you.

Remember, according to God, "every matter must be established by the testimony of two or three witnesses" (2 Corinthians 13:1).

So God is not offended when we test the spiritual urgings of our hearts. In fact, He is pleased when we do so. In the Bible, we are told to "prove all things" (1 Thessalonians 5:21, KJV). God is not upset when we "prove" Him. In the Bible, we are told to "try the spirits whether they are of God" (1 John 4:1, KJV). The work of the Holy Spirit is never "quenched" in our lives when we examine what He seems to be telling us by comparing those things with the written Word of God. Also in the Bible, we are told to pass judgment on those voices that seek to influence our lives (see 1 Corinthians 14:29). Therefore, God is not disappointed when we verify through the Bible those things that our hearts seem to be telling us.

In fact, God does not look at biblical confirmation as a sign of spiritual weakness; He looks at biblical confirmation as a sign of spiritual maturity and wisdom. The mature believer should never act upon any impulse of his heart until he analyzes that impulse through the lens of Scripture. God will never lead one of His children to do something that opposes the clear teachings of the Bible.

For this reason, you should not think of biblical confirmation as an expression of doubt toward the Holy Spirit. Rather, you should think of biblical confirmation as an expression of doubt toward yourself. It's not the voice of God that you are questioning, but rather your own ability to differentiate the voice of God from your own voice and from the voices of the people around you who are constantly trying to influence you in subtle ways.

I totally believe that God speaks to His people. After all, He is a living God, and He has been speaking since the very beginning. So why would He stop speaking now? I have seen the destruction that ensues when people respond impulsively to the "voice" they claim to hear in their hearts only to discover later that the voice they heard was not God's voice at all. It was a counterfeit voice that was disguised to sound like God's voice. It was the voice of their own subconscious desires or the voice of friends and relatives who were trying to nudge them toward a specific action. It was the voice of conventional wisdom or the voice of that person's own idealistic fantasies.

I trust God completely, but I don't trust myself. I don't trust my own ability to know the voice of God when I hear it or to differentiate His voice from the voice of my own subconscious mind. That is precisely why God gave us the Bible in the first place. It is our guide. It is a "lamp unto my feet, and a light unto my path" (Psalm 119:105, KJV). We would be absolute fools to leave our Bibles lying unopened on our nightstand when we need God's guidance the most.

That is why, when God has given me faith to embrace a miracle for my life, I begin to name that miracle. I begin to proclaim it and define it in my heart and my mind through precise verbal descriptions. I start praying about it, and I start believing that God will provide it for me. But then I pick up my Bible and start searching for that miracle in God's Word. If the miracle that God has planted in my heart is a legitimate miracle that God wants me to experience in my life, I will find that miracle somewhere in the pages of the Bible. I will find biblical evidence to support my miracle in the pages of God's Word. I will either find an explicit teaching that tells me God performs those kinds of miracles today, or I will find a biblical story that provides me with evidence that God has done something similar in the life of one of my spiritual predecessors.

Therefore, I won't need to pray any more of those "if" prayers. I won't need to pray, "If it be thy will, heal me." Instead, I can take hold of the biblical promise that "with his stripes we are healed" (Isaiah 53:5, KJV). I won't need to pray, "If it be thy will, bless me financially." Provided that I have been obedient to God in financial matters, He has made it clear to me that He desires "above all things that thou mayest prosper" (3 John 2, KJV). And I won't need to pray, "If it be thy will, help me overcome this terrible addiction in my life." Instead, I can pray with the apostle Paul that "the God of peace Himself sanctify you entirely" (1 Thessalonians 5:23, NASB).

The Bible contains inexhaustible wisdom about every subject that is relevant to living a godly life in an ungodly world. And it is obvious that God had to be the mastermind behind this magnificent piece of literature, because no mortal human being could have possibly created the content of the Bible. No group of human beings could have collaborated to produce the Bible.

Just think about it! What man could have written, "Husbands, love your wives, even as Christ also loved the church, and gave himself for it" (Ephesians 5:25, KJV)? The obvious answer to this question is that no man living at that time in human history could have written something like this, because no man would have thought this way. Or what woman could have written, "Wives, submit yourselves unto your own husbands, as unto the Lord" (Ephesians 5:22, KJV)? The obvious answer is that no woman living at that time could have independently written these words.

Only God could have imagined the text of the Bible. Only God could have given us 66 stand-alone books that were written by approximately 44 different human authors who produced their documents without the benefit of collaboration over a period of at least 1,500 years, and who did so while unwittingly creating one harmonious record that contains no factual errors, no contradictions, and hundreds of prophecies that have been fulfilled precisely as they were given at just the right moments in human history.

The Bible is no ordinary book; it is much more than a merely human book. It is the divine Word of God, given to us through supernatural means and preserved for us through supernatural methods. We are fools, indeed, if we ignore its knowledge or reject its wisdom or refuse to avail ourselves of its rich treasures during the times when it speaks most powerfully to our circumstances.

To know the Word of God, therefore, is to know the will of God. To know the Word of God is to know the mind of God. So naming my miracle is the vital first step toward realizing a miracle in my life. But unless I confirm the miracle I am naming by validating it through the Word of God, my faith for a miracle can be misdirected and my faith for a miracle can be without basis. A genuine miracle will always find its origins in the written Word of God.

When I was young, my mother used to have a little magnet on her refrigerator door, and the magnet bore a slogan that she frequently quoted and often repeated to me. The slogan simply stated, "God said it, I believe it, and that settles it." But God hasn't really said anything until He says it through His Word.

His Word is my only infallible guide for faith and conduct. It is my only reliable compass through the maze of life. That is why I often write on index cards those verses of promise that deal directly with the challenges I am facing in my life. I write them down, I put them in places where they are quickly available to me and readily noticeable, and I read them and quote them often as I continue to name my miracle and trust God to provide it. I do this because the Word of God is amazingly potent. It is astonishingly powerful. Sometimes, as Christians we get so accustomed to the Bible that we lose sight of its miraculous ability to shine light into our darkness or to inject life into something that has died in our lives. But the Bible can truly transform any person. It can resurrect and restore anything!

Some time ago, I listened to a powerful and moving sermon by my good friend of mine, Kendall Bridges, the lead pastor at Freedom Life Church in Carrollton, Texas. In fact, I don't believe I have ever heard a sermon on the subject of healing that moved my heart and stirred my soul quite like the sermon I heard him preach. But as I listened to his sermon a second time, I realized that it wasn't really a sermon at all. All Kendall was doing was reading scriptures about healing. He was simply repeating what the Bible had already said about the power of God to heal the human body, and those words stirred my passions and motivated my faith like nothing else could.

I have a friend who is helping me with some of the editorial work for this book, and he recently told me about a similar experience he had at a conference in the Midwest. He was attending a missionary conference in Missouri and suddenly a man walked out from behind the curtain (unannounced) and began to make his way to the front of the auditorium to address the hundreds of foreign missionaries who were attending the evening service at this international gathering. The man had a fake beard and disheveled hair, he wore sandals and clothing that were reminiscent of the Roman era, and he leaned upon a long staff as he made his way to the front of the auditorium to face the conference guests. Complete silence fell over the congregation.

Utilizing a concealed wireless microphone, he introduced himself as the apostle Paul. But after offering his brief introduction, this professional actor—in full costume—began to preach. It didn't take my friend very long to figure out that this actor had memorized the entire book of Ephesians and was repeating those 155 verses verbatim as if the apostle Paul were preaching a sermon to the believers in first-century Asia Minor. My friend told me that he had never experienced anything quite so powerful and so inspiring in his entire life.

It was the Word of God and nothing more. No elaboration! No explanation! Just the unvarnished words of the Bible! But my friend had never heard the words of Ephesians presented quite this way. He was moved in a manner that forever changed him. Indeed, the Word of God "is living and active. Sharper than any double-edged sword, it penetrates even to dividing soul and spirit, joints and marrow. It is able to judge the thoughts and intentions of the heart" (Hebrews 4:12, Berean).

So my second recommendation to you as you trust God to do something miraculous in your life is to search the Scriptures to know the mind of God and the will of God regarding the miracle you seek. If you need a miracle from God, begin to clarify that miracle in your own heart and begin to confess that miracle to the Lord as you name that miracle in your prayers and as you focus on it through your thoughts. But then present that miracle to the objective scrutiny of God's Word, which is designed to help you distinguish between the authentic will of God and your own wishful thinking.

If you find a clear teaching that demonstrates God's willingness to perform a miracle like the one you need, you will have your corroborating testimony. If you find a biblical example of God performing your miracle for someone who has preceded you in the faith, you will have your divine confirmation. But if you can find no biblical precedent for the miracle you seek, you really need to pray and lay your heart bare before the Lord so you can know God's will in the situation you are facing. Just because He has never done it before doesn't necessarily mean He won't do it for you. But knowing He has demonstrated that exact kind of power in times past can instill the faith that you need to face your personal challenge today.

CHAPTER 3

Request Your Miracle

**Ask God for your miracle,
seek him until he provides it, and knock until he
opens the door and grants your request.**

Once you have named the specific miracle you need from the Lord and once you have confirmed through the Scriptures God's willingness to provide it, you must begin to fervently pray for the miracle you desire.

Prayer has always been a mystery to me. If my heart desires something and God's Word says that I can have it, I don't fully understand why I need to ask God for it. But that's the way things work in the kingdom of God. That's why He is God and I am not God. He doesn't think like me—or like you. For some reason known only to God Himself, prayer is the necessary ingredient that gets things moving in the Spirit realm.

With my limited ability to grasp the mind of God, I cannot fully understand why prayer is so important to Him, but I do understand the importance of faith and passion in the Christian life. Perhaps that is why God wants us to pray. He wants us to pray so we can show Him that we really do mean business, that we really do mean what we say, and that we truly desire what we claim we desire. He wants us to pray so we can show Him that we really do believe He has the power to provide the miracle we request.

Passion has always been closely associated with answered prayer. James wrote, "The effectual fervent prayer of a righteous man availeth much" (James 5:16, KJV). Just notice the adjectives in this verse. The prayers that avail much are the prayers of a "righteous" man, a man who is absolutely serious about following and serving the Lord. And what kind of prayer will avail when a righteous man prays? An "effectual" prayer! A "fervent" prayer! I don't want to repeat the teachings of the previous chapter, but this just helps to validate what I wrote in chapter 2: God doesn't respond to "sissy" prayers. He doesn't like things that are lukewarm. Instead, God likes things either "hot" or "cold" (see Revelation 3:15). God responds to passion!

In case you still aren't convinced, start paying attention to some of the descriptions of worship and prayer that you find in the Bible. In Psalm 42, for instance, the writer proclaims, "As the hart panteth after the water brooks, so panteth my soul after thee, O God" (Psalm 42:1, KJV). A hart is a deer. So just picture this scene: A deer in the wild is thirsty. In fact, he is extremely thirsty. So thirsty, in fact, that his tongue is hanging from his mouth. He is panting for oxygen and for hydration. Then suddenly   he spots a water brook. How passionately do you think he is going to approach that cool, refreshing water? How passionately do you think he is going to drink? This is how the writer of this psalm saw himself worshipping the Lord. As a deer pants for fresh water when he is thirsty, so the worshipper pants for the Lord. Nothing else really matters when one is starving for either water—or the Lord's presence.

We can see this kind of spiritual passion in Jesus. On the night before He died—the night when He prayed His one and only "if" prayer in an effort to change God's mind about the crucifixion—Jesus prayed so passionately that "an angel from heaven appeared to him and strengthened him" (Luke 22:43). But then, Jesus kicked it up a notch. He actually "prayed *more earnestly*, and his sweat was like drops of blood falling to the ground" (Luke 22:44, emphasis mine).

I'm not saying that you have to pray until blood drips from the pores of your skin. But I am trying to show you that the prayers that command the attention of God are those prayers that are marked with passion, with spiritual hunger and thirst, with deep fervor and excitement, and with a sense of urgency that will not be denied. These are the prayers that move mountains, move God, and move situations in our lives. These are the prayers that count.

But you might be amazed at how many Christians don't know they are supposed to ask for the things they need from the Lord. These Christians just assume that God will provide the things they need. Nevertheless, God often waits for us to pray before He responds to the desires of our hearts. In fact, He often waits for us to pray earnestly, passionately, and for an extended period of time before He acts.

James, the brother of Jesus, said, "Ye have not, because ye ask not" (James 4:2, KJV). So if you haven't received the miracle you have named and confirmed, then perhaps it's because you haven't asked God for that miracle. Perhaps you need to pray, and perhaps you need to pray passionately, persistently, fervently, and with some fire in your belly and your soul. Perhaps you need to shed some tears and lift your voice so God cannot possibly ignore you. Perhaps you need to wrestle with God the same way that Jacob wrestled with the Lord on the banks of the Jabbok River (see Genesis 32:22–28).

During his earthly ministry, Jesus certainly taught us to ask God for those things we desire from him. Again, this doesn't make any sense to me. My natural mind cannot appreciate God's wisdom in such matters. In my limited way of thinking, if God knows the very thoughts of my heart, then He knows what I am thinking and He knows what I need from Him. So why do I need to pray? Why do I need to tell Him what He already knows?

But it is not my place to question the wisdom of the one who made me. It is not my place to second-guess His ways. It is my place to believe Him and obey Him. So I must listen to the Savior when He commands me to "ask, and it shall be given you; seek, and ye shall find; knock, and it shall be opened unto you" (Matthew 7:7, KJV). In these familiar words, we once again recognize the attitude of persistence that really moves the heart of God. We recognize the attitude of determination that stirs God to action. For some reason that is beyond my comprehension, God really likes it when His people, driven by a sense of desperation, beat down His door in the middle of the night and refuse to go away until He answers them. But believe it or not, that is exactly how God wants us to approach Him.

In Luke 18, "Jesus told his disciples a parable to show them that they should always pray and not give up" (Luke 18:1). He told them about a fictitious judge in a certain town who resisted the efforts of a local widow to obtain justice from him against her adversary. But when the judge refused to grant the woman's request, the woman just continued to annoy the poor judge. She continued to petition him with her demands. And eventually the judge responded to her, not because her demands were particularly worthy, but simply because she would not go away. And that is the way Jesus told His disciples that they should approach God. That is the way Jesus taught His disciples to pray.

But that was not the first time Jesus had taught this lesson of prayerful persistence to His disciples. In Luke 11, we read about an occasion when Jesus returned to His disciples after spending His own personal time in prayer. The disciples, admiring Jesus' prayer life, asked Him to teach them to pray. And that is when Jesus taught them the Lord's Prayer.

But immediately after giving His disciples the wonderful template for the Lord's Prayer, Jesus hammered home the need for tenacity in prayer, and He made this point strongly by means of another parable. Jesus said, "Suppose you have a friend, and you go to him at midnight and say, 'Friend, lend me three loaves of bread; because a friend of mine on a journey has come to me, and I have no food to offer him'" (Luke 11:5–6).

In the parable, Jesus explained the unwillingness of this neighbor to get up in the middle of the night and respond to his friend's request. In fact, the neighbor apparently yelled at his friend from his bedroom window, telling him to go away. "Don't bother me," he said. "The door is already locked, and my children and I are in bed. I can't get up and give you anything" (Luke 11:7).

But Jesus revealed to His disciples His "secret" for a successful prayer life when He said, "I tell you, even though he will not get up and give you the bread because of friendship, yet because of your shameless audacity he will surely get up and give you as much as you need" (Luke 11:8). According to Jesus, therefore, boldness and persistence are two of the most important prerequisites to answered prayer, and "shameless audacity" is the "secret ingredient" that makes certain people's prayers so effective. The man who will not hold his tongue and go away is the man who will get what he needs from the Lord. In other words, when it comes to prayer, "the squeaky wheel always gets the grease."

If you want to receive the miracle you are naming and the miracle that is confirmed in the Word of God, you have to ask for it. You have to ask for it passionately. You have to ask for it persistently. You have to refuse to take "no" for an answer. If you don't get your answer the first time you knock on God's door, you need to knock harder. Then you need to ring the doorbell and wake up the dogs. You need to blow your car horn in the driveway and throw rocks at the bedroom window. You need to make such a nuisance of yourself that God will give you what you want just to get rid of you.

Once again, I don't understand any of this. God didn't confide in me or seek my advice when He wrote the eternal laws of His kingdom. But I do know from my lifelong study of God's Word and my lifelong experience of walking with Him that this is the way He does things., He responds to faith. He is moved by passion. He is stirred by boldness. He is influenced by persistence.

For example, look at the woman with the issue of blood. We are told in the Bible that this woman forced her way through the crowd and reached out to touch the hem of Jesus' garment. This woman was not passive; she was active. In fact, she was aggressively active. She had a need, and she was not about to let anybody keep her from making her way to Jesus and receiving the miracle that she needed from Him.

It's the same way with the paralytic in Capernaum. The paralytic's friends refused to let the crowd or the circumstances keep them away from Jesus. When they could not get their paralyzed friend close to Jesus because of the large crowd that had gathered around Him, they simply climbed on top of the house where Jesus was teaching, cut a hole in the roof, and lowered their friend's pallet, with him on it, down to Jesus.

And the list goes on and on. Jairus, the Roman centurion, the nobleman from Capernaum, and others who sought healing for their servants and their children often traveled many miles to plead with the Savior to come with them to heal the person in need. The syrophoenician woman refused to take "no" for an answer when Jesus compared her to a dog, so Jesus finally complimented her faith and threw her "some crumbs from the table" by healing her daughter of demon possession.

Parents brought their children to Jesus, who was often in the wilderness or in a community far from where they lived. And you know that Jesus knew about these people. He was the Son of God, so He knew everything and He could have healed their diseases and deformities from far away. But Jesus waited for the people to come to Him. He waited for the people to find Him. He waited for the people to walk long distances, to endure the heat and the sun, to go without food until He had to feed them, and to find creative and assertive ways to fight their way through the crowds in order to get close to Him, touch Him, and make their requests known to Him. In short, Jesus waited for these people to show some desperation and some passion before He responded to their needs.

Unfortunately, this biblical directive to approach God with audacious and persistent prayer can present a problem for some people, because some people need a miracle from the Lord, but they do not feel worthy of the miracle they seek. And it's impossible to be bold and persistent when you don't feel worthy of receiving what you are requesting. Make sure you resolve the issue of your own worthiness before you start praying and fasting for a miracle.

The fact of the matter is that many Christian people walk around beneath a cloud of unworthiness, and this is one of the primary reasons we don't see more miracles in our lives. Miracles come only to those who boldly and persistently demand them through prayer. But boldness and persistence come from a sense of entitlement. So when a believer feels that he is unworthy of God's goodness or grace, that believer won't do the things that are necessary to obtain God's favor in his life. He won't pray. He won't beat down heaven's door. He won't persist in prayer through faith.

This is why confidence is so closely aligned in the Bible with answered prayer. This is why the Bible says, "When you ask, you must believe and not doubt, because the one who doubts… should not expect to receive anything from the Lord" (James 1:6–7).

Confidence is the hidden quality that gives a person assurance of his forgiveness and his acceptance by God. Confidence is the hidden quality that gives a person the ability to believe that God hears him and will respond to his pleas.

A person with confidence knows that he has failed God at times, but he also knows that he has been forgiven and that God thinks highly of him. A person with confidence knows that he often falls short of the glory of God, but he also knows that he has been made whole through the blood of Jesus Christ and that he has become a child of God. Because of his intimate relationship with God through Christ, he walks in favor with God and he realizes that his life is filled with blessings. Because he is God's child, he is a privileged member of the family of God and he possesses a rich inheritance that has been bestowed upon him by his heavenly Father.

David was not a perfect man, but he was a spiritually confident man. David wrote, "I remain *confident* of this: I will see the goodness of the LORD in the land of the living" (Psalm 27:13, emphasis mine). David, though flawed by sin, knew without a doubt that he would partake in the resurrection from the dead. Paul, too, was a spiritually confident man. Writing to one of his most impressive churches, Paul said, "I always pray with joy… being *confident* of this, that he who began a good work in you will carry it on to completion until the day of Christ Jesus" (Philippians 1:4–6, emphasis mine).

The person who knows his position "in Christ" and his position in the family of God is the person who won't hesitate to approach the throne of God in prayer when he has a need. He is the person who will feel comfortable entering God's presence to present his requests to the Lord. As the apostle Paul explained to another first century church, the person who is confident in his standing with God will be able to approach God "in boldness and access with *confidence*" (Ephesians 3:12, KJV, emphasis mine).

Just a couple of days before His death, Jesus was teaching His disciples about prayer's direct connection with confidence. In that conversation Jesus said, "Whatever you ask in prayer, believe that you have received it, and it will be yours" (Mark 11:24). In other words, you won't receive much of anything from God unless you believe that God has already decided you should have it. And you won't believe that God has decided you should have what you are requesting from Him unless you believe you are worthy of receiving it.

When Jesus told His disciples about the necessity of faith in the process of prayer, Jesus wasn't telling His disciples that they needed to believe in *God* in order to receive their requests; the disciples already believed in God. And Jesus wasn't telling His disciples that they needed to believe in *God's ability* to do supernatural things; the disciples had already witnessed enough miracles to fill the four gospels that they would write in the years to come. Instead, Jesus was telling His disciples that it was necessary for them to believe that God would actually do miraculous things in response to their individual prayers, that God would actually do things for them the same way God had done things for him.

So Jesus was saying that another essential ingredient for answered prayer is belief in one's own prayers. To receive a miracle from God, you must believe that God is there and that He is listening to you, and you must believe that He is powerful enough to grant your request. But beyond that, you must also believe that God wants you to have what you are requesting and that you are worthy of receiving that blessing from His mighty hand. If you don't believe these things, you won't receive anything from the Lord.

If you truly believe that God wants you to have the miracle that is resonating within your heart, then you are halfway to the finish line. You are halfway to the realization of your dream. Your prayers will take on a different nature. They will take on a different attitude.

Instead of acting like a beggar, who sees himself as an unworthy recipient of the crumbs from someone else's table, you will begin to see yourself as a child of God, worthy of receiving God's favor through the blood of Jesus Christ. And your prayers will reflect this change in attitude as you pray with increased boldness and increased confidence. But as you engage in prayer for your miracle with this newfound boldness that God requires, please be aware of four factors that need to shape your prayers if you want to see them answered.

First, if you want God to answer your prayer for a miracle, you must learn to pray in a way that is not self-centered.

God loves you, and He wants to bless you and fill your life with good things. But please keep things in perspective when you pray to the Lord. Your comfort and happiness are not God's highest priorities. God's highest priority in the earth is to build a kingdom of redeemed souls who will worship and serve His Son throughout eternity. And God's highest priority in your life is to change you from glory to glory until the image of Christ is perfected within you. Although God loves you more than you will ever know, one of the primary reasons He has invested so much in your life is so that you can become His chosen vessel for impacting others on His Son's behalf. With this in mind, learn to pray in a way that will seek to honor Christ and that will seek to implement God's purposes in the earth. Don't focus your prayers exclusively on minimizing the momentary discomforts you may be experiencing in life.

When God was dictating the Old Testament law to Moses high atop Mount Sinai and the Israelites were worshipping a golden calf in the camp below, God told Moses what the people were doing and He told Moses that He wanted to separate Himself from the rebellious Israelites and establish a completely new nation through Moses. You can read the account of this intense conversation in Exodus 32:1–14.

But Moses prayed, and he changed God's mind on the matter. He changed the mind of God by appealing to God's high esteem for his own name. Moses could have easily taken advantage of this situation. He could have elevated himself and could have become the progenitor of his own great nation. But Moses passed on the opportunity. Instead, he made God's reputation the focus of his prayer, and he prayed for God to fulfill the promises He had made to the great men who had preceded him in service to the Lord: Abraham, Isaac, and Jacob.

"Why should the Egyptians say, 'It was with evil intent that (God) brought (the Israelites out of Egypt), to kill them in the mountains and to wipe them off the face of the earth'?" Moses asked. "Turn from your fierce anger; relent and do not bring disaster on your people. Remember your servants Abraham, Isaac and Israel, to whom you swore by your own self: 'I will make your descendants as numerous as the stars in the sky and I will give your descendants all this land I promised them, and it will be their inheritance forever.'"

Moses refused to take advantage of the situation by whining about his own personal struggles or his own personal challenges as a leader. He refused to take advantage of the situation by asking God for something for himself. Instead, Moses asked God to engage in an act of grace that would protect God's own name and confirm the eternal promises God had sworn in His name. He prayed for God's glory to prevail and for God's reputation to be upheld. It's amazing how often you find examples in the Bible of God's willingness to perform miracles when those miracles were directly attached to the petitioner's zeal for God's glory rather than his own personal needs.

In fact, almost every miracle that Jesus performed was a miracle attached to a divine purpose rather than a human purpose. Yes, Jesus delighted in alleviating human suffering, and He delighted in blessing those who loved Him and believed in Him. And yes, the recipients of Jesus' miracles were definitely enriched as a consequence of the miracles he performed. But Jesus was more interested in building the kingdom of God and completing the mission God had sent Him to fulfill than in handing out favors to His followers.

Jesus turned the water into wine, not simply to meet the immediate needs of those attending the banquet, but also to reveal his own glory and to inspire His disciples to believe in Him as the Son of God (see John 2:11). And Jesus told His heavenly Father that He wanted to raise Lazarus from the dead, not only for the benefit of Lazarus and his two sisters, but also to inspire faith in the hearts of those who would witness this mighty deed and in the hearts of those who would hear about it. Jesus told the Father that He wanted to raise Lazarus so that people might "believe that you sent me" (John 11:42).

King David asked the Lord to forgive him for the sin of adultery and to restore him in every way, not only for David's benefit and blessing, but also that David might "teach transgressors your ways, so that sinners will turn back to you" (Psalm 51:13).

If you look closely when you read the Scriptures, you will notice that almost every miracle in the Bible has a greater purpose than merely meeting a temporary human need. Almost every biblical miracle contributed to achieving a particular divine purpose in human history. Learn to pray from God's perspective as much as you pray from your own, and learn to look out for God's interests as enthusiastically as you look out for your own interests. Every time you pray for a miracle, ask yourself, "Why would God want to perform this miracle for me? What purpose can this miracle achieve beyond the satisfaction of my own temporary needs?"

I am not saying that God doesn't care about your earthly needs, because He does. God doesn't want you to suffer or to worry or to fail or to die. But I think that God will be much more inclined to respond to your requests for a miracle if you can demonstrate that your miracle serves a greater and more eternal purpose than simply rescuing you from a difficult situation.

Remember, God is concerned about both worlds—the natural world and the supernatural world. He is concerned about Heaven and Earth at the same time, because He created both the spiritual world and the material world.

As a believer, you need to be concerned about both worlds, too. You need to pray for your own temporal needs, because God is concerned about your legitimate earthly needs (see Matthew 6:8). But you also need to pray with eternity in mind. You need to present a bigger picture to God than merely a picture of your own short-sighted comforts. Once God knows that your perspective has been enlarged, He will be much more inclined to show you His favor.

Second, if you want your miracle to become a reality, you must learn to "see" your miracle in your own heart as you pray for it.

Before you ever see your miracle in the physical world, you are going to have to start seeing that miracle through the eyes of faith. Most of us have to "see" something in our mind's eye before we can believe it, and we have to believe it before we can achieve it. What are you believing for your future?

Whenever I find myself asking God for a miracle, I begin the journey toward the realization of that miracle by trying to "see" my miracle in my own heart and mind. If I am trusting God to save an unbelieving relative, for instance, I close my eyes when I pray and actually visualize that person sitting beside me in church or lifting his hands in worship. I visualize the fulfillment of the thing I am asking God to provide.

If I am asking God to restore someone's marriage, I try to visualize the kind of marriage I know that person would like to have. I try to picture the person arriving home after work and entering a home that is filled with love and joy, as well as the sounds of laughter and the smells of good home cooking. If I am praying for a healing in someone's life, I try to picture that person doing things he or she cannot do at the present time. I picture that person running or jumping or skiing or wrestling with the grandkids on the living room floor.

One of the most effective pathways into the world of the miraculous is the pathway that makes it possible to "see" the miracle before it actually occurs. David Yonggi Cho pastors the world's largest church, located in Seoul, Korea. When his church was in its infancy, Dr. Cho would often preach with his eyes closed. He didn't do this to avoid looking at the members of his growing congregation; he did this so he could "see" in his mind's eye, not just the people who were there at the time, but the thousands who would join them in the months and years to come.

Dr. Cho didn't invent the power of visualization. Actually, God invented it, and he employed it often to help build faith in the hearts of his people. Take Abraham for example. God spoke to Abraham and told Abraham that He would bless him and make his name great. God spoke to Abraham and told Abraham that He would give the land of Canaan to him and his descendants forever and that He would bless the nations of the earth through him and his offspring.

Abraham believed God when God made these amazing promises to him. That is what made Abraham such a great man. He was able to believe and trust the Lord in spite of how things looked at a particular moment in his life. But Abraham was human, like all of us, and there were times when his faith was challenged and when his confidence grew weak. That's when God would step in to build up Abraham's faith. It was one of those times of personal weakness when God spoke to Abraham and said to him, "Hey, Abraham, look up at the sky for a moment, and tell me what you see."

"I don't see anything, Lord," Abraham responded. "It's nighttime, so there are no birds up there. There's just a lot of stars. A whole lot of stars!"

"Well," God responded. "Let that picture soak into your brain, because that's a picture of your future. You are going to have as many descendants as there are stars in the sky. If you can count the stars, then you will be able to count your offspring."

I'm paraphrasing, of course. But you can read the precise words of this conversation in Genesis 15:1-6. The thing to note here, however, is that God was building Abraham's faith by helping Abraham visualize his future. He was trying to give Abraham a "picture" of what his miracle would look like when it was finally developed.

Then God took the illustration further when He said, "Hey, Abraham, how many grains of sand are there on the seashore?" (the actual conversation can be found in Genesis 22:17).

"More than I could count," Abraham said.

"Well, that's another picture of how your descendants are going to look in future generations," God said. "Nobody can count the grains of sand on the seashore, and nobody will be able to count your offspring."

So God was teaching Abraham to "see" his miracle before he actually *saw* his miracle. God was teaching Abraham to visualize the thing he was requesting in prayer and trusting God to supply.

Jesus also promoted visualization and imagination when He encouraged His followers to look at natural things in order to understand spiritual things. Jesus pointed to clouds to help His disciples grasp the reality of future events. He pointed to children to help them grasp the concept of humility. He pointed to mustard seeds to help them understand faith. He pointed to fishing nets to help them understand soul winning. Jesus regularly used physical things that people could see to help them understand spiritual things they could not see.

Learn to use the things that you are familiar with to help you focus on the miracle you have not yet realized in your life. Draw a picture in your mind of the way you want things to be, and then hold onto that picture as you pray and believe and confidently trust God for the miracle you desire. If you can "see" it, you can believe it. And if you can believe it, you can obtain it!

What is the miracle you are seeking? What is that one thing you want God to do in your life? Right now, I want you to stop reading for just a moment and close your eyes. As soon as you finish this paragraph and the next one, I want you to put down this book and take a few moments to simply visualize the end result of the miracle you need from God. I want you to picture yourself or your loved one or your situation the way you want it to be after your miracle has come to full fruition.

If you are praying about a new business, I want you to visualize that new business and get a clear picture of the office, the parking lot, and even your business card. If you are praying about a restored marriage, I want you to picture yourself with your spouse, and I want you to picture that scene exactly as you want it to be after God injects himself into that situation. If you need a healing, picture yourself doing things you cannot do right now. If you need a financial break-through, picture the things your newfound money can provide for you and your family. And if you need a better job, picture your new executive suite with the sign on the door and the secretary sitting outside your office. Just stop for a moment and picture it!

Through visualization and imagination, give life to your miracle in your own heart and mind so you can have something tangible to hold onto while God works in the spiritual world to make your miracle a reality in the physical world. The physical world is comprised of matter, space, and time, therefore, it will probably take some time before God gives substance to your request. But until it becomes real in the physical world, it can be real right now in the spiritual world. It can be real in your heart.

The "me" I see is the "me" I will be. So if I see myself prosperous, healed, triumphant, and successful, then that is the person I will become as long as I do the things that are necessary to contribute to that outcome. And if I can "see" those outcomes in my heart, God will do the part I cannot do while I do the part that I *can* do. And that is the basis for a miracle.

Learn both the power and the limitations of visualization. While visualization cannot make something a reality when it is not a reality, visualization can help something that is real take shape in your heart and mind while God is giving that thing substance in the material world. And while visualization alone won't create something out of nothing (we refer to this kind of thinking as "fantasy"), visualization that is based on the promises of God's Word can be a powerful tool that keeps the visionary on track and keeps him focused on his dream when there is nothing yet tangible within his grasp.

According to the Bible, "faith is the substance of things hoped for, the evidence of things not seen" (Hebrews 11:1, KJV). Therefore, faith has the ability to "see" something before it exists, and faith has the ability to give shape to something before it can be felt or weighed. But while fantasy pretends that something unattainable might somehow happen anyway, genuine faith knows for sure that something genuine is on its way.

Third, after you have learned to pray with God's best interests in mind and after you have learned to visualize the miracle you seek, become willing to do your part to answer your own prayer.

Read your Bible and you will notice that Jesus spent a lot of time praying. He also spent a lot of time talking about prayer and teaching His followers *how* to pray. On one occasion (in the Garden of Gethsemane), Jesus actually invited His disciples to join Him in prayer. But during His lifetime, the Lord shared only one prayer *request* with His followers. Only once in His life did Jesus ask others to join Him in prayer regarding something specific that was important to Him. He told His disciples to "pray ye therefore the Lord of the harvest, that he would send forth labourers into his harvest" (Luke 10:2, KJV).

Jesus wanted His disciples to pray that God would send laborers into the spiritual harvest fields of the world. But when the disciples finally took up this prayer request later in their lives, they are the ones who became the workers in the harvest fields for which they prayed. They became the answer to their own prayers.

The best way I can describe a miracle is to tell you that a miracle is the supernatural thing that God does after you and I have done all the natural things that we can do in the physical realm. A miracle is the part of the equation that God takes upon himself—the part that only He can do—after we have taken upon ourselves the part of the equation that we *can* do.

In fact, almost every time Jesus worked a miracle, He began by requiring those who would benefit from the miracle to do something that was easy for them to do. And when they obeyed the Lord by doing the thing He commanded them to do, He did something supernatural in response to their obedience.

For instance, when Jesus was at the wedding feast in Cana and when He learned from His mother that there was no more wine in the house, Jesus told the servants there to bring Him the six empty water jars that were in the house. He told them to fill the jars with water. Then He told them to dip out the water and take it to the master of the banquet. After the servants had done everything Jesus told them to do, Jesus did the rest. He did the part they could not do. He performed a miracle!

When Jesus' disciples came to Him, informing Him that He needed to dismiss the five thousand people who had followed Him into the countryside and send them back home so they could find something to eat, Jesus discovered that there was a young boy in the crowd who had two fish and five small loaves of bread. Jesus told His disciples to bring the fish and bread to Him. Then He told the disciples to organize the people into groups and distribute the food. Notice that after the disciples had done everything Jesus told them to do, Jesus did the rest. He did the part they could not do. He performed a miracle!

This is the usual pattern that Jesus employed whenever He performed a miracle in somebody's life. When He healed the invalid at the pool of Bethesda, He told the man to pick up his mat and carry it home (see John 5:1–9). When He raised Lazarus from the dead, He told those who were there that day to roll the stone away from the entrance to the tomb (see John 11:38–39). And when He healed the man who had been born blind, He rubbed mud in the man's eyes and told him to go wash himself in the Pool of Siloam (see John 9:1–7). Almost always, Jesus gave an "instruction" before He actually performed the miracle that was needed in that particular situation. He required the people to do their part before He would do His part.

This pattern is not limited to the New Testament or to the ministry of Jesus. In the Old Testament, God parted the Red Sea only after Moses extended his rod over the waters (see Exodus 14:15–16). God parted the Jordan River only after the Levites picked up the Ark of the Covenant, placed it on their shoulders, and set their feet in the rushing waters (see Joshua 3:13). God gave an almost endless supply of flour and oil to the starving widow at Zarephath only after the widow gave the last of her food to the prophet Elijah at his insistence (see 1 Kings 17:13–14). God leveled the walls of Jericho only after the Israelites marched around the city seven times at the Lord's command (see Joshua 6:2–5). And God healed Naaman of leprosy only after Naaman dipped himself seven times in the Jordan River according to the word of Elisha (see 2 Kings 5:1–10).

Are you getting this? If you want a miracle in your life, you have to pray for God's purposes to be fulfilled through that miracle, you have to "see" that miracle in the deepest recesses of your own heart, and you have to do your part in the natural realm to make that miracle a reality. If you are faithful with your itty-bitty part, God will be more than faithful with His great big part. He will do the part you cannot do.

This reminds me of a section of the Colorado River where people go to enjoy whitewater rafting. I've never been there myself, but I've been told that you must sit through a short course on rafting before they will allow you to climb into the raft with the rest of the people and make your way down the river. During the course, the instructor explains that if you should somehow fall out of the raft into the rushing waters, someone will rescue you. But you must become "an active participant in your own rescue."

This is great advice, not only for rafters, but also for those who want God to rescue them from troubled waters. God does indeed work miracles in this day and age but there must be legitimate faith to support the miracle, and there must be a legitimate need to give rise to the miracle. In addition, there must be a legitimate effort on the part of the believer to do everything in his power to give life to the miracle he desires.

If you need a miracle in your life, God will almost certainly instruct you to do something to bring forth that miracle and to position yourself for a manifestation of His power in your life. Be obedient to the Lord and faithful with the little things He has placed in your hands to do. If you will do your part, God will do His part. He will do something to inspire awe in your soul and to absolutely amaze those who are standing on the sidelines, watching to see whether your faith has any substance (see Matthew 15:31).

Fourth, when you pray for your miracle, refuse to give up.

Once again, one of the things about God that fascinates me is the way He thinks. He just doesn't think the way I think. He just doesn't do things the way I would do them if I were in His position (an extremely frightening thought). For instance, if I were God, I would give a person one opportunity to present his request to me. Then I would weigh that request on its merits and either deny it or grant it accordingly. But God responds to faith, not logic or persuasive arguments, and faith is often best exhibited through persistence. The person who truly believes in his own prayers will persist in his prayers.

We have already analyzed this subject at some length, but at this point in our discussion I would like to more fully explain why I believe that prayer is the most potent weapon in the Christian's arsenal. I would like to explain why prayer truly has the power to move mountains. For example, if the average person were required to define prayer, that person would probably join the *New Oxford American Dictionary* by explaining that prayer is "a solemn request for help or expression of thanks addressed to God or an object of worship." And I guess that's a fairly accurate depiction of prayer from a purely secular point of view. But to me, prayer is much more than that. In fact, in my personal "dictionary of spiritual truth," I would define prayer as "the only thing in the universe that has the power to change God's mind." That's right! Prayer can actually compel God to change His mind.

Just think about that! Prayer is much bigger and it has played a much more prominent role in human history than you might imagine, because prayer alone has the power to change God's thinking, to change God's actions, and to change God's plans for our lives. I can give you multiple examples from the Bible to support this perspective on prayer, but let's take a look at a few of them.

God worked a miracle for Hezekiah when God caused the shadow to move backward on the stairway. That was one of the most amazing miracles in the Bible, because God either had to reverse the rotation of the earth or He had to bend light in order to make the shadow on the stairs move backward. Either way, this miracle represented a temporary suspension of one of the most fundamental laws of the physical universe. For a moment in time, God "postponed" the laws of physics that hold our universe together, and He did it specifically to fulfill a divine purpose. But why would God do this? What was it that motivated God to do such an amazing thing?

In approximately 700 B.C., King Hezekiah of Judah became ill and found himself at the point of death. At God's command, the prophet Isaiah went to Hezekiah and told him, "This is what the LORD says: 'Put your house in order, because you are going to die; you will not recover.'" You can read the full account of these events in 2 Kings 20:1–11.

But Hezekiah prayed. In fact, he prayed with passion and with a sense of urgency. He turned his face to the wall, and he prayed until the tears flowed down his face. And his prayer apparently touched God in a big way. In fact, that prayer touched God so profoundly that God spoke to the prophet Isaiah again before Isaiah had even left the palace courtyard. God told Isaiah, "Go back and tell Hezekiah, the leader of my people, 'This is what the LORD, the God of your father David, says: I will add fifteen years to your life. And I will deliver you and this city from the hand of the king of Assyria. I will defend this city for my sake and for the sake of my servant David.'"

Hezekiah's prayer actually changed the mind of God. Amazing! When Isaiah went to Hezekiah to tell him he was going to die, Isaiah said, "You will not recover." There was no uncertainty in that message. God was not showing any indecision. The Lord had made up His mind; Hezekiah would die. The time had come for Hezekiah to leave this world and to stand in judgment before God. It was a sealed deal. But something happened to change God's mind. Hezekiah prayed, and God totally reversed the course. Does the power of that thought impact you the way that it impacts me? God changed His mind, and He changed His mind simply because one man prayed.

Then God worked a series of mighty miracles. He caused the shadow to move backward on the stairway to confirm that Hezekiah's prayer would be answered, He healed Hezekiah completely, and He sent an angel to miraculously kill 185,000 Assyrian soldiers who were encamped around the city of Jerusalem (see 2 Kings 19:35). I can't recall a time in the biblical narrative when God worked so many miracles so rapidly for anyone. And all this happened because Hezekiah prayed one little prayer!

Yet, this is not the only time that God changed His mind as a result of prayer. As we saw earlier in this chapter, Moses managed to change God's mind when he stood between the Lord's righteous anger and the guilty Israelites who had fashioned an idol out of gold. In fact, the word *intercession* means "to stand between two parties and represent the interests of one to the other." Moses stood as an intercessor for the people of Israel. God wanted to abandon the Israelites and establish a completely new nation through Moses, but Moses prayed until God changed His mind.

On still another occasion, God had plans to destroy Sodom and Gomorrah but Abraham learned about God's plan and interceded for those cities. As a result, God decided that He would not destroy Sodom and Gomorrah if only ten righteous people could be found there (read the full account of Abraham's prayer in Genesis 18). And even though "the LORD had closed Hannah's womb" (1 Samuel 1:6), Hannah prayed and convinced God to alter His plans for her life by giving her a son. And Samuel was born.

If you think about it, prayer is nothing more—and nothing less—than an effort to change the mind of God. When you pray, you are asking God to look at the circumstances He has handed to you in life and then to change those circumstances simply because of your request. Now I know that prayer involves more than this. Sometimes prayer involves worship. Other times, prayer involves thanksgiving or repentance. But most of the time, prayer involves intercession for others (asking God to change something in their lives) or supplication for ourselves (asking God to change something in our own lives). Prayer, therefore, is primarily an endless effort to convince God to change His mind about something He has allowed in our lives or in the lives of the people we know.

For this reason, it is important to persist in your prayers. Don't give up. Don't ever give up. When you go to the Lord in prayer because you need a miracle in your life, God can only respond to you in one of three ways: He can say "yes," He can say "no," or He can say "wait." If He says "yes," then tomorrow's prayer should be a prayer of thanksgiving. But if God says "no" or "wait," then tomorrow's prayer should be the same prayer you prayed today. Persist in that prayer until God changes His mind or until you change yours.

Be aware, however, God does say "no" sometimes. We can see this in the life of David, especially in the events that transpired following David's adulterous affair with Bathsheba. Bathsheba was married to a soldier named Uriah but had an affair with David while her husband was fighting in the siege of Rabbah. When David learned that Bathsheba was pregnant with his child, he ordered the commander of his army to send Uriah to the front lines of the siege so Uriah would be killed in battle. Then David quickly married Bathsheba in an effort to make it appear as if the child had been conceived on their wedding night. Through the prophet Nathan, however, God confronted David for his sin and told David that the child he had conceived with Bathsheba would die. When the baby was born, he was indeed stricken with a life-threatening illness.

In the face of this dire situation that seemed remarkably similar to the one Hezekiah would face some 300 years later, David fasted and prayed in an effort to change God's mind. He got on the ground, and for seven days he "pleaded with God for the child" (2 Samuel 12:16). But on the seventh day, the child died anyway. God said "no."

Nobody knows why God changed His mind for Moses and changed His mind for Hezekiah, but why He refused to change His mind for David. Nobody knows. But it's not our place to know the thoughts of God. They are too lofty for us to understand. Instead, it is our place to pray. And when God finally answers, it is our place to trust Him.

David's reaction to God's final denial of his prayer tells us everything we need to know about David and his character. David's reaction tells us exactly why God elevated this man so highly in spite of his temporary fall from grace: "Then David got up from the ground. After he had washed, put on lotions and changed his clothes, he went into the house of the LORD and worshiped. Then he went to his own house, and at his request they served him food, and he ate" (2 Samuel 12:20).

David praised God even when God said "no," because he trusted God's wisdom and God's goodness. But David would not quit asking God to change His mind until the final verdict had been rendered and the sentence had been carried out. You also should persist in prayer regarding the miracle you are seeking until God either says "yes" or "no." Who knows if God will listen to you and change His mind? Prayer is a powerful thing!

Be aware, however, that God is never in a hurry. When it comes to prayer, you and I are always in a hurry, because everything is urgent from our perspective. In fact, we don't usually start praying about something until it becomes a crisis in our lives. But God is never in a hurry. That's another reason you should "pray without ceasing" (1 Thessalonians 5:17, KJV).

God's perspective of time isn't the same as yours and mine. God has all of eternity to accomplish His purposes; haste never accompanies His actions. When God makes you wait for an answer, just keep praying. As Jesus said, keep praying and keep beating on the door until God grows weary of your constant requests and rises from His bed in the middle of the night to give you what you want.

Prayer is a lot like the ripples in a swimming pool. Years ago, I was alone in a community pool early in the morning. I was just lying there, with my entire body (everything except my face) immersed in the cool water as the sun was rising over the horizon. While I was lying on my back, staring up at the slowly brightening sky, I was wiggling my fingers beneath the surface of the water and slowly moving my hands back and forth so I could feel the soothing flow between my fingers.

After a few minutes, however, I heard some water splashing at the other end of the pool, so I lifted my head out of the water to take a look around. I thought somebody else had entered the pool to enjoy the early morning sunrise. But nobody was there. The noise was being caused by the little waves that were splashing against the concrete wall at the other end of the swimming pool.

I thought, *Where did those little waves come from? What caused them? The water was perfectly placid when I entered the pool and settled back to enjoy the sunrise. What made the water start splashing?* Then it occurred to me that I had created those waves with my own hands. I created currents beneath the water that had traveled the entire length of the pool to collide with the concrete at the other end. My own hands and arms had caused those ripples. I was barely moving, but that constant back-and-forth action had set forces in motion beneath the surface of the water that eventually produced a noticeable reaction at the other end of the pool.

Through this experience, God showed me a vivid correlation between the physical world and the spiritual world. In the same way that the persistent movement of my arms caused a chain reaction in the water that eventually resulted in some rather sizeable waves at the other end of the swimming pool, my prayers will eventually result in a sizeable manifestation in my life if I will just keep praying. My arms set invisible physical currents in motion beneath the surface of the water, and my prayers set invisible spiritual forces in motion the moment I begin to pray. But in the same way that it took time for the ripples to travel the length of the pool and manifest themselves by breaking against the wall at the other end, it will take time for God to manifest a physical response to my prayers and make His response evident in the natural world.

Therefore, be patient. Keep praying. Don't give up. Hang in there. If you have real faith, you won't abandon your miracle. One of the reasons God will sometimes make you wait for an answer is to separate the genuine prayer of faith from the short-term request for comfort. He wants to see if you really desire the miracle you are seeking from Him, and if you really have the faith to trust Him to provide it.

This reminds me of the time a woman approached me after a Sunday-evening church service and said, "You know, I prayed one time for six months, asking God to give me a van. I needed a new van badly, so I prayed and prayed. I asked God to provide that van for me, but He never did."

I asked her, "For six months? You prayed for six months?"

"That's right," she replied. "Every single day for six months. But God never answered my prayer."

"Did it ever occur to you that God might have given you that van in the seventh month?" I asked.

"No, I didn't think about that," she responded.

So I told her, "You may have given up right on the brink of your miracle."

I wonder how many Christians fail to see miracles in their lives because they give up and walk away before their miracles can be brought to life. I wonder how many people fail to see God's mighty strength manifested in their lives because they abandon the pursuit of their miracle just when God is beginning to take them seriously. On Judgment Day, when all things will be exposed and all things will be brought into the light, I wonder how many of us will discover that we were just one inch away from a miracle when we stopped praying, stopped believing, or stopped doing our part to receive a miracle from the hand of God.

As I have explained, prayer and faith are mysteries to me. I am still learning about them every day as I put faith into practice and learn to pray with more passion and more persistence. But this much I know: I know that, for whatever reason, God usually does not do things in the Spirit realm until somebody prays. He waits for us to pray before He heals us, even though it is His will to heal (see Exodus 15:26). He waits for us to pray before He forgives us, even though it is His will to forgive (see 1 John 1:9). He waits for us to pray before He sends people into the highways and byways of life to share the Gospel with those who need it (see Matthew 9:38), even though it is His will to redeem lost souls.

God's part is to do the miraculous; our part is to pray. But when we pray, God often will move heaven and earth to respond to our requests, especially when we pray with fervor and with a holy determination.

CHAPTER 4

Confess Your Miracle

**Say the same thing about your miracle
that God is saying to you through your heart
and through his Word.**

The Bible tells us that "death and life are in the power of the tongue" (Proverbs 18:21, KJV). You have probably heard this scripture before. But what did God mean when He inspired the writing of these words? And how does this biblical truth apply to your life, especially when it comes to miracles?

The best way to understand the relevance of this statement to your life is to take a look at some of the most accomplished people in history and the role that words played in their achievements. For example, on the positive side, let's look at the Kennedy family. Few families have made a greater impact on our nation and our world over the past century than the Kennedys. For sixty-four consecutive years, one of the members of this family held elective office in Washington, DC. Even though some people may disagree with the political positions espoused by the Kennedys and while others may object to the lifestyle they seem to promote, nobody can deny the influence this family has had on our nation and on recent history.

But what is it about the Kennedys that has set them apart? What has caused them to be such consistent over-achievers? Most of the Kennedys attended Harvard, and many of them have held high elective office. One was president, one was attorney general, three were senators, and it seems like all of them are millionaires.

There are many factors that have contributed to the success of the Kennedys, providing them with an almost irrepressible passion for doing ambitious things. But one of the primary factors that has contributed to their individual and collective success is the fact that they have a family tradition of talking about personal dreams and noble ideals when they sit around the dinner table as a family.

Even when they were young, the Kennedy children (Joe, Jack, Rosemary, Kathleen, Eunice, Patricia, Robert, Jean, and Teddy) were influenced and motivated by the grand visions for their family and their country that were expressed when all of them were together. The children were told that they were "great," and they were raised to believe that they were no ordinary children. They were raised to believe that each of them had a personal destiny that would lead them to do great things. And the family expected great things from each of its members.

So the Kennedy children grew up believing that they were "special," not in an arrogant way, but in a way that recognized their individual abilities and potential. They were raised to believe that each of them had a purpose in this world that nobody else could fulfill, and that each of them had the talents and the necessary support to realize their dreams. Because of the positive, uplifting, and visionary verbiage that flowed from their father and mother and because of the example set for them by their parents when it came to the pursuit of their dreams, these children grew up believing that they could do grand things and make a significant difference in the world. So they did!

At the same time, you can see the negative influence of words by looking at some of the world's most notorious scoundrels. Mass murderers like Ted Bundy, Jeffrey Dahmer, and Charles Manson were typically abused as children, both physically and verbally. They were frequently told that they were worthless. They were often told that they were evil. Their parents would even say to them, "I wish you had never been born."

Many family members today are abusive toward one another, if not physically, then at least verbally. Sometimes words can leave a more painful wound and a more enduring scar than a blow from a fist or an open hand. Sometimes words can permanently shape the life of a child in a negative way, resulting in poor self-esteem that manifests itself through a lifetime of bad choices and destructive behaviors.

Personally, I believe the tongue is the most powerful force in the world. I believe it is much more constructive than all the efforts of all the scientists in the world combined. And I believe it is much more destructive than all the weapons of all the nations of the world combined.

Just think about it! Every war can be traced back to the tongue. Perhaps those wars were fought by soldiers and won with advanced weaponry. But the origins of any war are always traceable to an escalation in divisive rhetoric that mobilizes the competing factions into a state of heightened animosity that can only be resolved through bloodshed.

For instance, before the American Revolution began in 1775, great writers and orators arose to shape the thinking of the American colonists and to plant and propagate the seeds of revolt that gave rise to the war. Thinkers like Benjamin Franklin and Thomas

Paine and orators like Samuel Adams and Patrick Henry ignited the flames of freedom within the hearts of the American people. Once these words had given birth to a growing consensus for liberty, war was inevitable. And so was the outcome of the war.

The inverse is true, as well, because evil is fostered by words the same way that liberty is fostered by words. Long before World War 2, for instance, Adolph Hitler was influenced by the words of Friedrich Nietzsche, the noted German philosopher who was anti-American and anti-Semitic in his beliefs. And long before Iran became an Islamist state, the people of that country were heavily influenced by the writings and the speeches of the Ayatollah Khomeini, who lived in France prior to the Islamic Revolution of 1979.

Every great achievement of man has been preceded by words of inspiration and encouragement that have flowed from the great writers and speakers who have paved the way for these notable achievements. And every despicable act of man has been preceded by words of anger and prejudice that have flowed from the diabolical writers and speakers who have laid the groundwork for man's most shameful deeds.

Words are never neutral. Words always make an impression and leave their mark. They are more powerful than any weapon devised by man; they are more enduring than any institution. They are more helpful; they are more harmful. They are more constructive; they are more destructive. Words are the most potent force for good or for evil that God has ever placed at man's disposal. That is why God will hold us accountable for every idle word that flows from our lips (see Matthew 12:36). Our words are either true or they are false. They either heal or they kill. They either impart life or they impart death. So choose your words wisely, and use them with discretion.

Your words don't just affect others; your words also affect you in a very big way. Your words affect your feelings. Your words affect your thoughts. Your words affect your attitudes. Your words affect your behavior. In fact, there is a popular anonymous quotation about the power of words that has been the focus of many posters and many framed pieces of art. The quotation says:

Watch your thoughts, for they become words.

Watch your words, for they become actions.

Watch your actions, for they become habits.

Watch your habits, for they become your character.

Watch your character, for it becomes your destiny.

You can see how the words of your mouth can have a direct impact on the outcome of your life. Your speech patterns, therefore, are more than just a minor matter; they are the *heart* of the matter. They are extremely important, and they can definitely shape the course of your life.

King Solomon warned us when he said, "Death and life are in the power of the tongue." But also referring to the power of words, Jesus added, "Out of the overflow of the heart, the mouth speaks" (Luke 6:45, Berean). So which is more important, our words or our attitudes? Which one affects the other? Do our words affect our attitudes, or do our attitudes affect our words? Which came first, the chicken or the egg?

Actually, both of these statements are true. My attitudes shape my words, but then my words shape my attitudes. The words that come out of my mouth are manifestations of the "life" or the "death" that already exists within me. On the other hand, the words that I speak over and over can definitely impact the way that I feel about the subject I am addressing. So to me, my mouth is a monitor that can help me know the true condition of my heart at any given time. It is an alarm that can make me aware when my heart needs some spiritual attention. But at the same time, my words refortify the condition of my heart and bolster the attitudes that those words reveal. So if I find myself backbiting or complaining or making excuses for myself or placing blame at the feet of others, that is the Holy Spirit's due notice to me that I need to take inventory of my thoughts and feelings and do something to adjust them. But at the same time, my negative and derogatory words can inflame the anger, the prejudice, or the unforgiveness that I am already feeling in my heart. So my words are both a symptom and a cause of my heart's condition.

One of the most effective things I can do, therefore, to modify my thoughts about something is to purposely change my speech about it and start speaking positive words about that situation even before I start "feeling" the sentiments I am verbalizing with my refocused words. I can start speaking positive words about those people who have disappointed me or offended me. I can start speaking positive words about those problems that are raising the stress levels in my life. I can start speaking positive words about the miracle I am expecting from the Lord and positive words about the good outcome I am anticipating in that situation.

My tongue is a barometer of my spiritual condition. It is a gauge that alerts me when something is wrong inside. It also is the place where God's medicine is best applied to my life and where He often begins the healing process for my heart. By intentionally and deliberately speaking positive words, uplifting words, encouraging words, and life-giving words to others and to myself—even when I do not fully practice the words that I speak—I can start changing the climate of my environment, improving a sensitive situation, healing a damaged relationship, or restoring life to my own soul. With the right words spoken at the right time and in the right way, I can actually change myself, change others, and change my circumstances.

Think back over your life. How often, when you were a child, did you feel incapable of doing some of the things that were required of you as you made the transition from childhood to adulthood? As a child, you faced a great number of challenges that you might not think about today. You had to endure your first day at school. You had to pass difficult tests in your classes. On occasion, you had to stand up and speak to your fellow classmates. At Christmastime and at the end of the school year, you had to perform in front of a live audience. When you played Little League baseball, you had to stand at the plate and face the opposing pitcher in front of a crowd of noisy and critical parents. You had to pass your driving test when you turned sixteen, and you had to go out on your very first date.

Even in childhood, you faced a lot of challenges and a lot of frightening situations. Obviously, these were great moments in your life. In fact, they were pivotal moments that shaped you more than you probably realize. They were opportunities to grow and opportunities to learn. But they were frightening experiences too, because each one of these watershed moments in your life was a moment that could have ended painfully. There were no guarantees as you embraced these rites of passage. There were no assurances that things would go the way that you wanted them to go.

Wasn't it nice during those momentous occasions when your mother or father or some other adult would look at you and say, "You can do this"? Wasn't it comforting and strengthening to hear the words, "You're going to be fine"? Positive words have a way of lifting the spirit, encouraging the heart, and giving strength to the bones. They have a way of imparting life and drawing the best out of us. But your own self-talk—the words that you say to yourself when nobody else is around—is far more important and carries far more weight than any words that any other person could ever say to you.

If you are telling yourself, "I can't do this" or "God can't do this," then you are right. You can't, and He can't. No matter how persistently other people might try to encourage you or uplift you with their positive words, your negative self-talk will erase any positive things that God or other people speak over you. But the opposite is true, as well. If you are telling yourself, "I *can* do this" or "God *can* do this," then you are right again. You can, and He can. No matter how persistently other people might try to discourage you or put you down with their negative words, your positive self-talk will overrule any negative things that these people say to you.

Your words will impact the miracle that you are requesting from God, because your words will reflect your attitude toward that miracle and toward God's ability to provide it. Your positive words will reveal an attitude of faith and trust; your negative words will reveal an attitude of doubt and disbelief. And we all know that God only performs miracles in an environment of faith.

Your words also will have a direct bearing on the actions you take or refuse to take to make your miracle a reality. As I explained in the previous chapter, you must become a participant in your own miracle. There is something that God will require of you before you can see your miracle in the physical world. But if you doubt your miracle, you won't do what you need to do in the natural realm in order to prompt God to respond with reciprocal action in the spiritual realm. You won't act, because you don't truly believe that the miracle will occur. So you must learn to speak to yourself in a way that builds up your own faith. You must learn to speak in a way that nurtures the seed of faith within your heart.

Now let me take a moment here to explain something to you that is extremely important, because there is a great deal of superstition out there about the power of the tongue. Allowing one negative comment to slip out of my mouth in a moment of weakness or carelessness is not going to abort my miracle or destroy my life. Likewise, learning to recite all the right words is not going to assure my miracle for me, because my words alone do not have the power to force God to do something he is not inclined to do. So simply saying something out loud a couple of times isn't going to make that thing happen.

For instance, I can stand in my backyard all day long, look up at the sky, and say to myself, "I am a bird. I am a bird. I am a bird." But that won't make me a bird. Words only have power and they only have authority when they are rooted in truth, and truth cannot be altered simply because I experience an isolated slip of the tongue or start "claiming" something that isn't a legitimate demand on God's miraculous power. But words can certainly activate the truth in my life when I say them with conviction, and words can certainly make the truth irrelevant in my life if I refuse to acknowledge the truth that those words represent. My words can have power when my words become heartfelt confessions or become denials of the truths that I find in God's Word.

In fact, the word *confess* is a very strong and interesting word. Comprised of two syllables, the word has a very specific meaning. The little prefix, "con," comes from the Latin word meaning "with." And the root of the word, "fess," is Latin and French in its origins, meaning "to admit." So when I tell you that you need to "confess" your miracle, I'm not telling you to say something that is untrue until it becomes true. I'm not telling you to create something out of nothing with the sheer power of your repetitions. God's words have creative power, but man's words are incapable of calling into existence something that has no existence.

What I am telling you to do when I tell you to "confess" your miracle is to "admit with" God what He has already said about your miracle. If He has spoken to your heart, telling you that He wants to provide that particular miracle for you, then "admit" that fact "with" God. If He has shown you through His Word that He is both willing and able to perform the miracle that you seek, then "admit" that fact "with" God. "Say the same thing" about your miracle that God is saying about it. "Say the same thing" about your miracle that the Holy Spirit and the Word of God have confirmed to you to be true.

You cannot cause something to happen simply by saying it over and over out loud. But if God has said that something is possible, then that thing has a basis in reality. In fact, it is already a reality in the spirit realm. By "admitting along with" God that your miracle is possible and that God desires to provide that miracle for you, you can actually activate that miracle in your life. You can actually play a significant role in the provision of your own miracle.

Say the same thing about your miracle that God is saying about it. Has God shown you that He wants to provide that miracle for you? If so, "confess" that fact "with God." In other words, say the same thing about it that God is saying. Has God confirmed that miracle through his written Word? If so, then "confess" that fact. Say the same thing about it that God is saying. As you pray, "admit with" God that the miracle will take place. As you speak with other people of faith, "admit with" God that this miracle is going to happen in your life.

Do not misunderstand the power of confession. Confession is not saying something until it becomes a reality; confession is saying "with God" what He has already declared to be a reality. It is "admitting" what is already true. Confession is saying—along with God—the same thing that He is saying about the matter. It is reciting God's own words after Him, and that kind of speech has untold power.

By saying out loud the same thing about your miracle that God is saying about it, you are demonstrating faith. You are agreeing with the Lord. You are allowing your faith to express itself through the force of your very words. And for some reason, that is beyond my understanding, God is tremendously impacted by this kind of faith. In fact, nothing touches His heart or moves His hand quite like faith.

For instance, have you ever watched a father interact with his daughter? Nothing is sweeter than to see a loving father with his precious little girl. Those little girls come into the world preprogrammed with the knowledge of how to touch their fathers' hearts. Nobody teaches these little girls how to make their dads become putty in their hands; these innocent little children are simply born with this understanding.

If one of these little girls needs something from her father, she knows exactly what to do. She climbs into daddy's lap and gives him a great big hug and a kiss on the cheek. Then she stares at him with those big brown eyes, and daddy's heart starts melting like warm butter. He will willingly do anything she requests and gladly give her anything her heart desires.

I'm not saying that we should try to manipulate God because unlike human fathers, God cannot be manipulated. He knows "the thoughts and *intents* of the heart" (Hebrews 4:12, KJV, emphasis mine). But I am saying, however, that God has a "tender spot." Just as hugs and kisses can touch a father's heart, faith touches the heart of our heavenly Father. For some reason, faith really impresses Him, and faith stirs Him to action. He cannot ignore the presence of faith. Where He finds faith, He will move heaven and earth to respond to our prayers. Where He finds faith, He will move mountains to provide our needs. And faith is often most powerfully demonstrated through the words that we speak in response to God's own words.

But here's the truly amazing thing: This isn't a secret. God tells us this throughout the Bible. In a thousand different places and in a thousand different ways, He has shown us that faith causes Him to forgive sins, to pour out His blessings, to favor the faithful, and to perform miracles that can astound and amaze. Faith causes Him to take special notice of those who trust in Him and to leap into action when they cry for His help. Faith is the motivation that compels Him to act on our behalf.

If you know that God has spoken to your heart about a miracle He wants to perform in your life, if you have confirmed that miracle through the objective witness of God's Word, and if you have prayed earnestly and passionately about it, then start saying the same thing about your miracle that God has already said about it in your heart and in His written Word. Confess your miracle. Say along with God what He has already said about it. Agree with Him. Begin speaking positively and expectantly about your miracle to the Lord and to others who share your faith in the Lord. Talk about it as if it has already happened.

If you need a miracle in your body, for instance, speak about that healing as if it has already taken place. If you are trusting God to save one of your friends or family members, start confessing the person's salvation in your prayers and your everyday speech and visualizing that person worshipping beside you in church.

For example, if you are trusting the Lord to save your father, don't let the negative words of your mouth obstruct the faith that is in your heart. Don't go around saying: "Well, you know, I've been praying for my father for the past twenty years, and he hasn't given his heart to the Lord yet. It looks like he's never going to turn around. I think he's just too old and too set in his ways to change. I don't think there's much hope of him getting saved at this point in his life."

Instead, say the same thing that God is saying to you: "I can't wait until Dad gets saved. When he gets saved, it's going to be awesome. We're going to be able to go to church together and talk about the things of the Lord. Believe me! That day is coming soon. I can just feel it in my heart."

Can you see the tremendous difference between these two opposing attitudes? Can you "feel" the spiritual distinction between the expectant approach to a miracle and the skeptical approach?

God honors faith, but He rarely honors doubt or indecision. So make sure that God intends to supply your miracle, and make sure that you really need the miracle you seek. But if you know in your heart that you absolutely need a miracle—that there is no possible way to resolve your pressing problem without it, and if you know that God performs miracles like the one you are requesting—then pray faithfully for that miracle every day until it arrives. Also confess that miracle every day until it arrives. Say the same things silently to yourself and out loud to other people that God is saying about your miracle to you.

Remember, you are looking for your miracle and waiting for its arrival so you can leap for joy and give thanks to God. But God is looking for faith and waiting to find it in your heart and in your words so he can leap into action on your behalf and make that miracle a reality in your life. Begin to confess the miracle you are asking God to supply, the miracle you need Him to perform on your behalf. "Death and life are in the power of the tongue."

CHAPTER 5

Remove All Doubt

Protect yourself from the influence of people who do not share your faith in God's ability to perform a miracle in your life.

When the Israelites were preparing to enter the Promised Land, God directed them to do something that, on the surface, might appear to violate everything we know about God. God told the Jewish people to destroy everyone living in the land of Canaan. You can read the full text of God's command in Deuteronomy 20:16–18.

This command has always been a stumbling block for the unbelieving world and for many Christians as well. It is a part of the biblical narrative we would rather ignore. We prefer to think of God as grandfatherly. We prefer to think of Him as sweet. We prefer to envision a heavenly deity who is gentle, tender, merciful, and kind. It is difficult for us to reconcile our concept of a kindhearted God with a scene of utter destruction. How can we rectify this apparent contradiction in the nature of our God?

Unfortunately, a lot of Christians are one-dimensional in their faith, because they choose to see God through the narrow lens of their own personal needs rather than the lens of His self-revelation. They choose to fashion and shape God according to the way they want Him to be (idolatry) rather than the way He actually is (faith). In the Bible, however, where God reveals all sides of His multifaceted personality, our creator is indeed loving. In fact, He was loving enough to die for our sins. But He is also righteous. He is indeed patient, but He also makes it clear that He will not tolerate sin forever. The Lord can show abundant mercy, but He also has warned us that a day of reckoning is coming for all mankind, a day when He will weigh every man, woman, and child in the scales of justice. God beckons us repeatedly to hide our sins through faith in Christ, because we do not know the day or the hour of His visitation.

Consequently, the Bible teaches us to love the Lord, but it also teaches us to fear the Lord. In fact, we must fear God before we can properly love Him. The psalmist wrote that "the fear of the LORD is the beginning of *wisdom*" (Psalm 111:10, italics mine), and King Solomon added that "the fear of the LORD is the beginning of *knowledge*" (Proverbs 1:7, italics mine). Consequently, all spiritual wisdom and all spiritual knowledge flow from a healthy fear of the Lord. He is an awesome God, and His holiness demands a certain sense of reverence from those who approach Him.

Don't be surprised, therefore, that God called for the destruction of certain individuals and certain cultures in the days when He was prescribing His laws to the Israelites. And don't be surprised that today He calls for His people to be "separate" from those who disbelieve. Personally, I think God will be fair in all His judgments when men, women, and children stand before His throne to account for their lives. But I also believe that God is God, and I believe that God *believes* that He is God. So God believes that He actually has the right to call people to account for their sins and to reclaim their lives at His desire. After all, He gave them life, so He has the right to recall that life at any time and to demand an accounting for it.

In the Bible, God directed His people on many occasions and in many different ways to separate themselves from sin, from unbelief, from foolish behavior, and from spiritual rebellion. God told His people to be holy. In other words, to "set themselves apart" for the exclusive use of their God! Sometimes that call to holiness required stern measures, like the one mentioned above. At other times, God's call to holiness simply required separation by God's people from the undue influences of those who lived contrary to God's ways.

We don't like to think of God as being divisive. The god we prefer to worship (our mental idol god) always insists on unity and harmony. He always seeks peace and cooperation and camaraderie, regardless of the spiritual condition or beliefs of the people involved. He always reconciles and unites. He wants all the people of the world to take part in a great big group hug and then join hands to sing "Kumbaya" around the all-inclusive campfire of international respect and tolerance.

But such a vision of God is not biblical; this kind of vision is manmade, created for us and imbedded in our thinking by people who do not even know God. This is the idol god of modern popular culture. To the true and living God (the one revealed in the Scriptures), peace is a personal reality, not a condition of cease-fire among the world's warring factions. And love is something that God and his followers show to all people, even when they disapprove of the behaviors of the people that they love. But realizing that most people will never surrender to the true and living God or submit to His will or His ways, the Lord has commanded His people to manifest His love to everyone, but, at the same time, to set themselves apart from others in order to preserve their own spiritual health and to protect the sanctity of their own hearts.

God warned the Israelites that, if they failed to purge the Promised Land of all its heathen influences, they would be placing themselves in spiritual peril. They would eventually be spiritually infected by the sin of the surrounding nations, and they would lose their special destiny as God's chosen people. They would gradually turn away from God and gradually abandon the faith of their fathers. And the Jews did eventually lose their land to invaders due to the ever-increasing influences of idolatry and paganism that they failed to purge at God's direction.

God's command to "be separate" was not limited to the Jewish people. In the New Testament, God warned the church to do the same (see 2 Corinthians 6:17). And God warned individual believers to "be not unequally yoked with unbelievers" (2 Corinthians 6:14, ASV). The command for God's people to take reasonable steps to protect themselves from damaging spiritual influences is an ongoing command, a command of God for every day and every age, including ours. In the same way that command extends forward into the future, is the same way it extends backward to the creation of the world. Even before the first man existed, God was separating things.

Take a look for yourself. On the first day of creation, God "*separated* the light from the darkness" (Genesis 1:4, emphasis mine). On the second day of creation, "God made the vault and *separated* the water under the vault from the water above it" (Genesis 1:7, emphasis mine). On the fourth day of creation, God said, "Let there be lights in the vault of the sky to *separate* the day from the night" (Genesis 1:14, emphasis mine). And throughout the creation week, God made animals and plants "according to their various kinds" (see Genesis 1:11, 12, 21, 24, 25), a clear indication that there was an impenetrable boundary between the species, a wall of separation that could never be breached.

God does not always promote "oneness." Sometimes He actually demands "separateness." And to drive home this concept of separation, God required the Jews to purge their homes of leaven once a year during the Feast of Unleavened Bread. In the Old Testament, leaven was always symbolic of sin. Therefore, annually through means of a perpetual ceremony, God reminded the Jewish people that they needed to maintain a fearful respect for the power of sin and its hidden ability to influence their lives. They needed to purge sin from their hearts the same way that they purged leaven from their homes. They needed to eliminate sin's subtle influences on them the same way they that they eliminated leaven from those places where they lived, worked, and interacted with others.

God's people should think of sin as the moral flu. It is usually "caught" from other people. In the same way we can contract colds and influenza from the people with whom we associate, we can pick up the immoral behaviors and godless attitudes of the people who spread those contagions around. Like a virus, sin is often transferred from one person to another. This can be seen clearly in the very first sinful act in the Garden of Eden. Once Eve had taken a bite of the forbidden fruit, "she also gave some to her husband, who was with her, and he ate it" (Genesis 3:6). If it wasn't for Eve's encouragement, Adam may never have sinned.

God commands His people to be witnesses for Him among the unbelievers of the world. He commands His people to get close enough to others to demonstrate His love for them, to speak into their lives, and to influence them through positive attitudes and lifestyles. But God also warns His people to keep a respectable distance from those who can "infect" them. It is possible to love a person and spend appropriate time with a person without inviting that person into the inner circle of your life. To get too close and too familiar with someone who does not share your Christian values is to invite the contagion of sin into your own heart and mind.

Immorality is not the only spiritual quality that can be transferred from the unbeliever to the believer. Another quality that can be quickly and easily passed from one person to another is simple unbelief. People who lack faith have a powerful ability to destroy faith in the hearts of those who possess it.

It is hard to stand up for the Lord in the presence of people who don't believe in the Lord or acknowledge His Word. When a believer finds himself spending most of his time around callused unbelievers and when a believer invests most of his emotional treasure in building close relationships with those who mock his faith, that believer could easily become indifferent toward the Lord and could easily end up leaving the church in due time. But the person who forges most of his deep relationships with other like-minded followers of Christ is the person who will be able to stand strong for a lifetime even when circumstances require him to spend more time than he would like around people who profess no faith.

Here's a simple fact: No matter how strong you may be in your spiritual life, you need encouragement. You need to be built up in your faith. You need to see what God is doing in the lives of other believers so you can trust Him to do equally amazing things in your life. You need to hear the testimonies and exhortations of others who are walking through life victoriously so you can believe it is possible for you to do the same.

It's hard enough to live a victorious Christian life in this faithless world. As Christians, we are constantly called upon to walk according to principles and promises that have not yet fully materialized. We are called upon to obey commands when we cannot immediately see the value in doing so. If you add to this ongoing struggle the extra burden of dragging the negativity of your unsaved friends and relatives around with you, you are only going to slow your own spiritual progress and make yourself vulnerable to the enemy's attacks. Believe me, Satan's daily intent is to weaken you in every possible way so he can make your faith ineffective in your life.

This is why Jesus would not get too close to unbelievers. Yes, He visited unbelievers in their homes. Yes, He ate and drank with sinners, and He would even stop on the streets to talk with them and to minister to their needs (and we should do the same). Jesus would often heal a person without even inquiring about the status of that person's relationship with God. However, it's one thing to rub shoulders with unbelievers in a social or professional setting so you can make a positive impact on their lives, and it's another thing altogether to become intimate with those who cannot possibly understand the faith that motivates you. Jesus loved all people, but He would not entrust Himself to anyone, because He understood the sinful nature that drives men to do what they do (see John 2:23–25).

If you want to be successful in the Christian life, you are going to have to start building new friendships. Your best friends must be strong believers who can encourage you and help you in your Christian walk, and your relationship with your old friends must change. You should always love those people who do not yet know the Lord and you should reach out to them in every reasonable way, but you must be careful never to cast your pearls before swine (see Matthew 7:6). Unbelievers certainly need to hear the Gospel and see its impact on your life, but they cannot understand the deeper things of the Spirit and must never be placed in a position to counsel you or influence your Christian walk.

Likewise, if you intend to live the life of faith (a lifestyle that is necessary if you want to see miracles in your life), you must put respectable boundaries between yourself and those who do not believe in miracles. This means that you must not allow unbelievers to influence your thinking regarding God's ability to perform a miracle for you. But this also means that you may need to put some healthy distance between yourself and other Christians who, like the heathens of this world, do not believe in the miraculous power of God. And unfortunately, those kinds of Christians exist in every church. They can believe God to save their souls and to raise their bodies from a state of decay in the grave, but they can't trust God to raise their salaries or to heal their sicknesses.

In the same way that sin and unbelief are contagious, faith is contagious, too. When I was traveling with Benny Hinn, I attended healing crusades where I personally witnessed some amazing and inexplicable things. I saw people who had been crippled for years get out of their wheelchairs. I watched visible growths fall off people's bodies.

These things were not staged; they weren't fabricated. They were real. So why do things like this happen at a healing crusade, yet they rarely occur in everyday life?

Simple! At a crusade, there is an environment of expectancy—an environment of faith. Sometimes people travel for hundreds of miles to attend one of these crusades, because they desperately need a miracle. When you get thousands of people together under one roof who possess that kind of faith, there is nothing God cannot do in that atmosphere.

But I've seen the opposite occur, as well. I have seen some of these same people return home after a crusade with an undeniable testimony about God's miraculous power, only to fall under the evil influence of their friends and family members who questioned the miracle that occurred. These friends and family members would say, "Are you sure you are healed?

Maybe you just had an emotional experience that made you feel like you were healed. Or maybe you just got caught up in the excitement and you *think* that God did something in your life." In the same way that Satan placed doubt in Eve's heart with a simple suggestion ("You will not surely die"), these people know instinctively how to implant doubt in a person's heart and mind. Because of the sinful nature that controls their thinking, these people know how to snatch defeat from the jaws of victory. And then, as that doubt takes hold, the miracle begins to wane. With the first pain or the first sign of weakness, the person who received the miracle begins to doubt that the miracle even happened, and the person again succumbs to an attitude of helplessness and weakness. And soon, the sickness that God took away begins to return and to resume its control over that person's life.

Your surroundings matter when you are trusting God for a miracle. Your associations matter when you are trusting God for a miracle. If you hang out with people who have faith, people who can trust God for anything that His Word confirms, then you are more likely to see the manifestation of God's miraculous power in your life, because your faith will be strong and your confidence in God will be resilient. But if you hang out with people who complain all the time and doubt God, people who constantly tell you what God *cannot* do in your life instead of what He *can* do, then your faith will diminish and so will your chances to witness a miracle.

One time while He was in Galilee, Jesus was called to the house of a man named Jairus. Jairus was a ruler in the local synagogue, and his daughter was gravely ill. Jesus followed Jairus back to his house for the purpose of healing Jairus' daughter. Along the way, however, Jesus was detained by other people who were seeking miracles of their own, and He stopped to address those needs. Before Jesus arrived at Jairus' house, therefore, an entourage came to tell the Lord not to bother. The young girl had suddenly died.

Ignoring what they said, Jesus encouraged Jairus. "Don't be afraid," Jesus said, "just believe." And they continued the journey to Jairus' house.

"When they came to the home of the synagogue ruler, Jesus saw a commotion, with people crying and wailing loudly. He went in and said to them, 'Why all this commotion and wailing? The child is not dead but asleep.' But they laughed at him" (Mark 5:38–40).

So Jesus asked all of them to leave. That's right! He kicked every last one of them out of the house. Then He took Jairus, Jairus' wife, Peter, James, and John with Him into the room where the dead girl was lying. Jesus took the little girl by the hand and commanded her to get up. "Immediately the girl stood up and began to walk around (she was twelve years old). At this they were completely astonished" (Mark 5:42).

So even Jesus was discouraged and bothered by people who lacked faith. In fact, He specifically told His family members and childhood friends in His hometown of Nazareth that He could not do many miracles among them because of their lack of faith (see Matthew 13:58). The people of Nazareth just could not bring themselves to look beyond the familiarity of Jesus' humanity in order to trust His divinity. They just could not bring themselves to believe that Jesus could work a miracle for them. Jesus couldn't perform any miracles in Nazareth, not because he was incapable of performing a miracle, but because miracles only occur in an atmosphere of faith.

A similar thing happened to Peter in the book Acts. A few years after Jesus had ascended into heaven, Peter was called to the home of Tabitha (also known as Dorcas), a woman from Joppa who was well known within the church for her acts of kindness and her charity. It seems that Dorcas had fallen gravely ill and had died. Since Peter was nearby at the time, he was asked to come to the home.

When Peter arrived in Joppa, where Dorcas had lived, he went upstairs to the bedroom where the body was lying. "All the widows stood around him, crying and showing him the robes and other clothing that Dorcas had made while she was still with them" (Acts 9:39). Peter sent them all out of the room. Just like Jesus, he told all of them to leave. "Then he got down on his knees and prayed. Turning toward the dead woman, he said, 'Tabitha, get up.' She opened her eyes, and seeing Peter she sat up. He took her by the hand and helped her to her feet. Then he called for the believers, especially the widows, and presented her to them alive" (Acts 9:40–41).

I can't help but laugh just a little every time I read this story, because the text says that after Dorcas was raised, Peter called the "believers" back into the room. In other words, Peter had to force all the believers to leave the room in order to affect a miracle, because even the Christians in that community lacked the faith to believe that God could do something supernatural.

I'm sure they were faithful friends to Dorcas. In fact, they must have been good friends, because they were emotionally distraught at Dorcas' death. But these believers certainly weren't spiritually supportive in their friend's hour of need. They just could not believe that God could work a miracle for their dear friend, Dorcas. So Peter sent all of them out of the room. Like Jesus, he could not do anything miraculous in the presence of such overwhelming doubt.

Your friends matter. Your environment matters. The influences that pull on you all day long matter. Everything affects your faith, even if you are blind to its influence. And just because a person believes God for his salvation, that doesn't mean that he can believe God for a miracle. You have to choose your companions wisely. Especially when you need a miracle, you have to plant yourself in the midst of people who can encourage you and sustain you as you pray and patiently wait for the manifestation of God's power in your life.

I learned a long, long time ago that you can't shove a watermelon idea into a pea-sized brain. When I need a miracle in my life, I don't waste my time and precious energy trying to convince everybody around me that God can provide my miracle. I don't have the time to debate with them, and I don't have the energy to try to convince them of something their unbelieving hearts won't accept. There is a time to minister to others, but there also is a time to step aside and just let God deal with them until they learn what they need to learn and grow up spiritually. Besides, it's impossible to approach the things of God mentally, especially when it comes to miracles.

If I'm trying to start a new business and I need God to provide me with the necessary capital, I don't want to be around people who think I should flip hamburgers for the rest of my life. And if I believe that God is trying to take me to the next level in some area of my life, I don't need to hang out with people who just sit on the sofa all day, watching television and eating potato chips.

One thing I have always noticed about old friends is that all of them are content as long as everybody in the group stays where they are. But as soon as any member of the inner circle reaches for a higher rung on the ladder in an effort to pull himself up to the place God wants him to be, nobody will try to inhibit that step of faith more passionately than the person's old friends. Subconsciously your old friends don't want to see you grow, because that puts pressure on them to grow, too. They don't want you to change, because that puts pressure on you to change.

The people closest to you will often be the first to stand in your way when you try to pursue God's best for your life. And when you attempt to cross the invisible gulf between the natural and the supernatural, they will come out of the woodwork to discourage you and to deter you from your pursuits. Their lack of faith can deeply affect you when you are looking to God for new and better things for yourself.

When I was younger, I served as the senior pastor at a small church in Orlando, Florida. One night, a man who attended my church called me at home and said, "Pastor, I'm at the hospital. They have given my father just three days to live. But I don't believe it's time for him to go. I want you to come here to pray with me and to believe with me for a miracle in his life. I believe God can heal him, and I want you to come and stand with me in prayer."

How could I deny such an urgent and heartfelt request? So I got dressed (it was late) and went to the hospital. When I arrived, I was greeted in the hallway by this man's sister, who walked out of her dad's room and hugged me. "Oh, Pastor!" she said. "I'm so glad you came. Mom is going to be so relieved that you're here. You know, they have given my father less than three days to live. Any time now, he is going to meet the Lord. But just knowing that you are here will mean so much to my mother."

I listened carefully, and I appreciated the warm greeting and the gracious words. At the same time, however, my heart was troubled, because I didn't think I had been called to the hospital to comfort a grieving family. I thought I had come to pray the prayer of faith.

Then the man's brother came out of the room to greet me. "Pastor, thank you so much for coming," he said. "You know, they've given dad just a short time to live. In fact, he's unconscious right now and he can't communicate at all. But I bet he knows what's going on. And I know he'll be comforted by the fact that you are here with him during his final hours."

But again, I didn't think I had come to make funeral arrangements. I thought I had come to the hospital that night to ask God for a miracle. Then Mark, the man who had called me, came out of the room, and he was ecstatic when he saw me. "Pastor, I'm so glad you're here," he said. "Let's get in there and pray. I believe it's time for dad's healing. Let's get in there and pray right now."

Now that's what I came for! That's the kind of faith I was looking for when I arrived. So Mark and I walked into the room where his dad was lying. But as we were entering, I noticed that Mark's brother and sister were following us back into the room. So I turned around and asked them politely if they would mind giving Mark and me the opportunity to pray alone with their father.

"But we would like to join you," they said.

"I don't think that's a good idea," I replied. "Mark and I are going to pray for your father's healing. You believe he's already dead, and you're just happy that I'm here to be with the family in your time of grief. But the two of us believe that God wants to heal your father. So I would really appreciate it if you would give us just a moment of privacy with your dad."

Obviously, the brother and sister were offended by my words. But what could they do? They stood outside in the hallway and waited respectfully while Mark and I laid our hands on Mark's unconscious father and prayed for him. In this particular situation, I didn't have any choice. I had to create an atmosphere of faith in order to pray the prayer of faith. If I had allowed the rest of the family to stand there with me while I prayed, I would have been forced to pray a bland, milk toast kind of prayer that made everybody feel good, or I would have been forced to pray a passionate prayer of faith that I knew they were not supporting or truly believing in their hearts. So I followed the example set for me by Jesus and by Peter, and I politely asked them to allow Mark and me to have our moment of privacy with their father.

Three days later, when Mark's dad was supposed to be dead, he wasn't dead yet. A week later, he was still alive. Two weeks later, he was sitting up in his bed, eating and talking. And by the time three weeks had passed, the hospital had discharged him and sent him home. That was more than seven years ago, and Mark's father is still alive and doing well. Why? Because Mark and I separated ourselves from the doubters! We separated ourselves from those who lacked the faith to believe that God could do something to change their dire situation. Sometimes, you will have to remove doubt from your presence, too, if you expect to receive a miracle from the Lord.

Doubt is one of the most effective weapons the enemy can employ to keep God's people from realizing all the miraculous things that God has in store for them. And I have noticed that the enemy isn't limited to using unbelievers to spread that doubt around. He can use Christian people, as well, to spread the doubt that he cannot spread any other way.

Theoretically, other believers are supposed to be the firm foundation beneath our feet whenever we are walking through times of testing. In fact, James taught us to "call the elders of the church to pray" (James 5:14) whenever we should find ourselves in need of a miracle from the Lord. He explained that "the prayer offered in faith (by the church leaders) will make the sick person well" (James 5:15, parentheses mine).

In reality, however, believers can often be the last people to believe. Confessing Christians can sometimes become the strongest opponents to real faith. We see this lack of faith in Peter, who tried to deter Jesus from his appointment with the cross (see Matthew 16:21–23). We also see this lack of faith in Thomas, who refused to believe that Jesus had risen from the dead (see John 20:24–28). Perhaps this lack of faith in some believers explains why Jesus only took three of His disciples with Him when He went to the home of Jairus.

The church is full of thieves. That's right! The church is full of thieves. When I was younger, I thought the biggest problem with the church was the fact that there were sinners hiding in our midst. I thought that if we could only purge the sinners from our ranks, we would be holy in God's sight and powerful in the sight of man. But as I got older and gained more knowledge and experience, I realized that sinners weren't the problem in most churches. In most churches, the biggest hindrance to growth (numerical growth, financial growth, and spiritual growth) was the lukewarm Christians who had become content with a half-hearted approach to the teachings of the Bible. These are the "thieves" that I am talking about.

One of those thieves is "Mr. You Can't Make It." This guy makes his rounds within the church, robbing people of their visions and their dreams. He steals their hopes. He casts a dark shadow over the visions that God has placed within their souls. He also seeks to influence the church itself. "Our church shouldn't do that," he says. "That's too expensive. That's too much for us to handle. We're a small church, you know. We don't want to bite off more than we can chew. We can't do that. We can't make it."

When I am walking the pathway to destiny and pursuing the great things that God has for my life, I don't want to be around "Mr. You Can't Make It." I don't want to listen to his endless whining and all the reasons God cannot do a particular thing in my life. I don't want to hear him tell me why I shouldn't do this and why I shouldn't do that and how God is incapable of doing the improbable. If I am misguided, tell me so. If not, either encourage me or get out of my way. But this demoralizing song and dance that constantly focuses on the "impossibility" of the things that God wants to do in my life reminds me of the negative report given by the ten spies who persuaded the Israelites that it would be better for them to die in the wilderness than to fight for the destiny God had promised to them.

It's not the sinners who are infecting the church with disbelief; it's the church members. Too often, it's the people inside the church who are killing the church and obstructing the faith of those who want to put demands on the supernatural power of the Holy Spirit. Just think about it! Do you know any new Christians? Aren't they excited? Aren't they on fire for the Lord? Aren't they hungry for the Word of God? Aren't they aggressive in soul winning?

But now think about the people you know who are dry and stale in their faith. Quite often, it's the people who have been in the church the longest. And unless the people of God come to understand this natural tendency for believers to grow spiritually stale, those new, excited Christians are destined to become just as dry and ineffective for the Lord as their more experienced counterparts.

So surround yourself with people who believe. Surround your-self with people who understand the power of God and who accept God's ability to do great things in your life. As much as possible, stay away from those who openly mock your faith, and stay away from doubting Christians like "Mr. You Can't Make It" and "Ms. Good Enough."

She's the lady who discourages people from pressing "toward the mark for the prize of the high calling of God" (Philippians 3:14, KJV), because she likes things the way they are right now and she doesn't want anything to change. To her, everything is "good enough" the way it is.

Jude, the brother of Jesus, told those under his influence to build "yourselves up in your most holy faith" (Jude 20). It is up to you, therefore, to surround yourself with on-fire people, because nothing can build your faith quite like being around other people who pos-sess genuine faith. Faith is contagious, but doubt is contagious too. So choose which "infection" you want to contract.

Don't allow negativity to deter you from God's destiny for your life. Whether negativity arises from within or assaults you from without, deal with it as quickly as possible and as decisively as pos-sible. Get it out of your presence; get it out of your life. You have the power to choose your companions. You may not be able to control your environment 100 percent of the time, and you may not be able to control the actions or attitudes of everyone around you. But you do have the power to choose those people you allow to speak into your life, and you do have the power to choose those people you will allow to influence your thinking.

You also have the power to control the way you talk to yourself. You have the power to control your own attitudes and your own thinking. Every morning when you rise to greet the new day, you have a choice. You can choose to say, "Good morning, Lord" or you can choose to say, "Good Lord, it's morning." The choice is up to you.

Obviously, you cannot control your circumstances. And obviously, you cannot control what people think about you or what they say about you to other people. You cannot control your neighbors, and you cannot control the weather or the price of tea in China. But you *can* control yourself. And you *can* control your disposition toward life and toward the Lord.

When you wake up in the morning, you can choose to say, "Good morning, Lord!" You can choose to start your day with a positive attitude. You can choose to believe that God is going to help you deal with the weather and earn enough money to buy that Chinese tea.

You can begin your day with thoughts of faith. And you can begin your day with the belief that you can make it, that you can do it, that you can accomplish what you have determined to do. And as you embrace the Lord each day and celebrate His ability to do great things in your life, all those positive, faith-filled, victorious, more-than-a-conqueror thoughts will begin to shape your behaviors and directly affect the outcome of your life experiences.

On the other hand, you can choose to wake up each morning and say, "Good Lord, it's morning!" You can begin your day with negative thoughts, and you can carry those deathly thoughts of defeat around with you all day long. You can constantly remind yourself that it's raining outside, that your back hurts, that your boss is mean to you, that your kids are in a lousy mood, or that you'll never catch up on the work that is piled on your desk. While a more positive and thankful person might rejoice that he has a job and lots of work to keep him busy and to justify his employment, the person who has a negative outlook on life will just keep complaining about his work and everything else in his life.

All those negative thoughts will begin to dominate his thinking, and his thinking will dominate his behavior. Then, if he adds fuel to the fire by connecting with his negative friends at the end of his workday so they can moan and groan and whine and complain together, his whole life will become nothing more than an endless merry-go-round of negative thinking and negative feelings that lead to despair, frustration, and hopelessness.

So the choice is yours to make. You control what you say to yourself. You control the list of people who have the ability to speak into your life and influence your thinking. If you want to walk in the realm of the miraculous and if you want to see God's glory and favor in your life, you are going to have to erect reasonable boundaries between yourself and those people who are always trying to deplete your faith, deflate your joy, and talk you out of your hopes and dreams. You are going to have to fill your life with positive thoughts and with positive people who can help you get from where you are to where you want to be.

CHAPTER 6

Plant Your Seed

**You must plant an earthly seed
before you can reap a heavenly harvest.**

In chapter 3, we took a close look at the biblical connection between a miracle and faith-driven action. Almost always, God will require a person to do something to advance his own miracle before God will do the supernatural part to bring that miracle to life. To explain this biblical principle more fully, let's take a quick look at the original language of the New Testament, particularly the New Testament language as it relates to the miracles that Jesus performed.

I know you didn't buy this book to learn a foreign language, but most students of the Bible understand that the Scriptures were written before English became a real language. Sometimes, therefore, it is necessary to delve into the original languages of the Scriptures in order to fully understand the sentiments that the writers were trying to convey.

The New Testament was originally written in Greek. Therefore, to understand some of the subtler meanings of the New Testament that are not apparent in our English translations, it is helpful to explore the original intent of the Greek-speaking writers. With this in mind, it is interesting to note that, in the Greek language, verbs always have "moods." When the verb in a particular sentence appears in the *indicative* mood, for instance, that verb is simply making a statement: "I *throw* the stone." But when the verb appears in the *imperative* mood, that verb is communicating a command: "*Throw* the stone. Hurry up! *Throw* the stone now." In the Greek language, the original language of the New Testament, the word *throw* would be spelled differently in these two contexts.

I offer this brief lesson in New Testament Greek in order to make an important point here about miracles. The imperative mood, which is the "mood" of command, the mood that a drill sergeant would use when addressing his new recruits, is the mood that Jesus used when he started commanding those around him to do certain things to prepare for a miracle. Most of the time before Jesus performed a miracle, He would address His disciples in the imperative mood. And this is not the mood of "suggestion" or the mood of "recommendation." This is not the mood of a simple statement of fact. The imperative mood is the mood of forceful command.

For example, when Jesus turned the water into wine at the wedding feast in Cana, He told the servants there to "*fill* the jars with water" (John 2:7, imperative mood). Then He told them to "*draw* some out and take it to the master of the banquet" (John 2:8, imperative mood). And when "Sergeant Jesus" learned that there were five thousand hungry people but only five loaves of bread and two fish, He said to His disciples, "*Bring* them here to me" (Matthew 14:18, imperative mood).

Even through the word construction of certain Greek verbs, we can see that there is a definite "anatomy" to a miracle. A miracle consists of me doing my part in obedience to the Lord's command and God responding to my obedience by doing His part. It consists of me doing the natural part and God doing the supernatural part. It consists of my obedience followed by God's response to my obedience and prayers.

In this chapter, however, I want to pay special attention to the order in which these two events occur. We must do our part *first*; then God will do His part *second*. We must act or speak in faith; then God will *respond* accordingly. But faith must be exhibited before God will part the sea or raise the dead. And faith is most clearly exhibited by what we do, not by what we say or what we claim to believe.

In the New Testament, the apostle Paul had a great deal to say about faith. And in the New Testament, James, the brother of Jesus, had a great deal to say about works. Paul claimed that "it is by grace you have been saved, through faith—not by works" (Ephesians 2:8–9). But then James asked, "What good is it, my brothers and sisters, if someone claims to have faith but has no deeds? Can such faith save them?" (James 2:14).

Although it may appear that James and Paul are contradicting one another when it comes to the subjects of faith and works, both men are actually saying the same thing. Both men are saying that faith is the necessary element for salvation and for obtaining the favor of God, but genuine faith is best demonstrated through acts of obedience. Our actions best reveal what we truly believe in our hearts, so obedient actions are an outward sign of inward faith.

This is important in the context of our study of miracles, because every promise of God is conditional. In other words, every promise of God has a condition attached to it, a condition that must be satisfied before God will fulfill that specific promise in our lives. For example, God promised to perform miracles of healing and restoration, but only "if my people, who are called by my name, will humble themselves and pray and seek my face and turn from their evil ways" (2 Chronicles 7:14). God promised to forgive your sins and to reward you with eternal life, but only if you "believe in your heart that God raised (Jesus) from the dead" (Romans 10:9). And God promised that you could have whatever you requested from Him in prayer, but only "if you believe" (Matthew 21:22).

The next time you notice one of the great promises of God in the Bible, stop for a minute and examine the grammatical context of that promise. Somewhere in the context, you will find that important little word *if*. "*If* you do this, then I will do that." As individuals, we must meet the condition of God's promise; then God will apply that promise to our lives. But the opposite is true, as well: If we fail to meet the condition of the promise, we will fail to activate that particular promise in our lives.

I have said repeatedly that God *responds* to faith. And the key word here is the word *responds*. The *New Oxford American Dictionary* defines *respond* as "to act or behave in reaction to something." So God "reacts" to our faith. Faith must come first. It must come before God's reaction. God must see faith before He does anything for us. But once He sees faith, God "reacts" by doing those things that you and I cannot do. And how does God identify true faith? He identifies faith through the things we do, not the things we claim to believe. When it comes to faith, actions speak louder than words.

If you want God to perform a miracle in response to your prayers, you will have to meet the biblical criteria for that miracle. You will have to do your part first, and then wait for God to do His part in *response* to your faith. In a figurative sense, you will have to "plant a seed." In the world of agriculture, God would never allow you to reap a harvest first and then plant your seed later. In the realm of the supernatural, the same principle applies: God will not allow you to reap a harvest until you plant a seed. The seed comes first. God will give a harvest in *response* to the planting of the seed.

A "seed" can take on many forms. First, there is the "seed" of obedient action, as I have already explained. You must do your part of the miraculous equation *before* God will do His part of the miraculous equation. You must obey His "imperative" commands; then God will respond to your obedient faith by injecting Himself directly into your situation.

But another "seed" that God expects you to sow when you are seeking a response from Him is the seed of a sacrifice. Many miracles in the Bible were preceded with appropriate worship expressed through giving. And God looked upon these gifts as "seeds" of faith. People offered their sacrifices to the Lord because they were requesting and anticipating a return on their investment. They were expecting a greater gift from God than the one they were planting in the soil of God's kingdom. Consequently, their acts of giving became acts of faith.

There is something about seeds that you need to know if you hope to fully appreciate this biblical analogy. Most Christians are familiar with the biblical concept of "sowing and reaping," but there is one thing about seeds that few Christians ever contemplate: A seed is nothing more than future wealth in a tiny package.

Just think about it! A seed, if planted, has the capacity to give you what you need in the future. For instance, in just two to three months, one kernel of corn, planted in the ground, can put thousands of kernels of corn in your barn. A seed, therefore, more than any other object on earth, is actually a guarantee of future wealth.

But here's the challenge: While a seed of corn has the capacity to produce wealth for you in the future, that seed also has the capacity to produce gratification for you right now. So you can choose to be satisfied immediately by consuming your kernel of corn the minute you receive it, or you can choose to be bountifully blessed later by sowing that kernel of corn in the ground and waiting for a tremendous harvest. And if you can discipline yourself to wait for your harvest, you will be much wealthier tomorrow than you are today. Your inventory of corn will be multiplied hundreds of times over.

Money is the same way. Money can give you what you want right now. But to have what you want today, you have to consume your money today. If you can wait to consume your money, however, you can turn that small amount of money into a larger portion of money. For instance, if you can make yourself "sow" that money in some type of investment vehicle, you can be a lot wealthier in the future than you are right now.

A seed—whether a "seed" of corn or a "seed" of money—is future wealth in your hands. A seed has the capacity to satisfy you today. But at the same time, that seed has the capacity to make you much more prosperous in the future if you can convince yourself to turn loose of that seed and to plant it in soil that will allow it to release its potential. This can be difficult to do, however, especially when you are hungry or desperate, because planting a seed and waiting for it to produce its yield can take a lot of time.

If you have a seed, therefore, you already have enough in your hand to create everything God has destined for you in the future. You can create the food that you need for the future, and you can create the money that you need for the future. But to enable that seed to release the full harvest that is within it, you have to find the resolve to turn loose of that seed and to bury it in the soil.

So if your seed is a kernel of corn, you have to believe that you would be better off in the future by putting that seed in the ground than you would be by consuming it right now, because that hope alone can motivate you to plant your seed instead of devouring it. Likewise, if your seed is money, you have to believe that you would be better off in the future by putting that seed in the bank than you would be by spending in today, because that hope alone can motivate you to invest your money instead of wasting it on things you could really do without.

A Christian, therefore, who wants to reap the harvest of a miracle in his life has to believe that he can derive a future benefit by planting a seed in the kingdom of God rather than consuming that seed for his immediate gratification, because a harvest of any type is a product of faith. The farmer has faith in the laws of agriculture, the investor has faith in the laws of economics, and the believer has faith in the promises of God. A person's "seed" is simply the implement that he uses to express his faith in the laws of God. That person releases his seed and plants his seed so that, in the future, the reward will be greater than the immediate benefits of consuming that seed today.

But why can't God's people grasp this simple concept? When it comes to agriculture, we "get it." And when it comes to investing, we "get it." But when it comes to sowing a seed in God's kingdom with the expectation of a return on our investment, we don't always "get it." We say we "get it," but we don't really "get it." If we did, we would give to God more regularly and more generously.

In reality, however, giving is more than just a spiritual investment. It is more than just a monetary sacrifice for the kingdom of God. Yes, giving is similar to farming and similar to investing in the sense that it is the practical thing to do for one's future. But giving also has an element of worship attached to it, so giving is both an act of faith and an act of worship. It is an act of faith because it is an investment in the belief that, by giving to God, we can multiply His blessings in the future. But it is an act of worship, too, because the giving of that seed, especially in the midst of a personal trial, is a bold statement to God that you esteem Him more highly than yourself and that He is more important to you than your own temporal needs.

What you hold in your hand is a "seed"; what God holds in His hand is a "harvest." If you become willing to plant your seed, God will be willing to honor your step of faith and your act of worship by returning to you the harvest that you desire. But as you ponder this biblical truth, never forget three of the irrefutable laws of harvesting that God has given to us through his Word.

First, in both the physical world and the spiritual world, people sow seeds in expectation of a specific harvest.

When people plant corn, for instance, they plant corn because they want to harvest corn in the fall. When people plant tomatoes, they plant tomatoes because they want to pick tomatoes in the summer. Nobody plants corn and expects to harvest wheat, and nobody plants tomatoes anticipating a big harvest of grapes. People sow seed in expectation of a specific harvest. This is true in the physical realm, and this is true in the spiritual realm.

When Israel was struck with a plague that claimed 70,000 lives, King David purchased the threshing floor of Araunah so he could present an offering to the Lord for the specific purpose of halting the plague (see 2 Samuel 24:11–25). When the widow at Zarephath was confronted with starvation during a terrible famine, she gave the last of her flour and oil to the prophet Elijah for the specific purpose of obtaining an almost limitless supply of flour and oil for herself and her son (see 1 Kings 17:7–16). And God himself sowed a "seed" for a specific purpose when He gave His one and only Son so that Jesus might become "the firstborn among many brothers" (Romans 8:29 ESV).

David wanted God to stop the plague, so David gave an offering for that purpose. The widow needed food to eat, so she gave an offering for that purpose. In the Bible, people routinely presented offerings to the Lord with the expectation that God would do something specific for them in return. God, Himself, respected this same formula. When He wanted to create a great spiritual family of redeemed men and women in the earth, He gave an offering for that specific reason. He gave the offering of His one and only Son.

Consequently, in this chapter I want you to consider doing something you may never have done before. I want you to give thought to an appropriate seed you can offer to the Lord for the specific purpose of activating the miracle that you need in your life. I would agree with the assessment of many who believe that miracles are less frequent in the church today than they were when the church was in its infancy. I believe that one of the reasons for this decline in the frequency of miracles is the loss in this modern era of the concept of planting a sacrificial seed in the soil of God's kingdom in expectation of His divine intervention.

Second, in both the physical world and the spiritual world, every seed contains an invisible instruction.

If you could open a tomato seed and peer deep inside its construction with your naked eye, you would find a unique DNA code that sets that seed apart from every other kind of seed in the world. Likewise, if you could open an orange seed, you would find a different DNA code there, a code that is unique to the orange seed. The DNA molecules within each seed contain a specific "instruction" that causes that seed to reproduce a tree or shrub just like the one it came from. No seed ever gets confused, no seed accidentally gives life to the wrong kind of plant, and no seed ever produces the wrong type of fruit. God has programmed every seed with the unique and specific instructions that seed will need to do its work and fulfill its created purpose.

We see this concept in the opening verses of the Bible, where we read the account of the creation of the very first plants and animals. In Genesis 1, we read multiple times how God created the various forms of plant and animal life with the capacity to reproduce "according to their kinds" (see Genesis 1:11, 12, 21, 24–25). Each "seed," therefore, had a specific instruction to produce more life forms like itself. No seed had the capacity to produce alternative forms of life.

The same principle applies in the animal kingdom and even among human beings. You are the product of your mother's "seed" and your father's "seed." You bear many of your parents' features, because their genetic code has been reproduced in you through their "seed." If both of your parents were dark skinned, then you are dark skinned. If both of your parents were light skinned, then you are light skinned. In both the plant kingdom and the animal kingdom, the composition and traits of every biological life form are predetermined by the genetic code of the "seed" which gave that thing life.

This principle also holds true in the spiritual world. As I explained earlier, God determined long before he created the heavens and the earth that He wanted to have a family of redeemed people in the earth. But when sin separated God from the people He had made, He took a "seed." In fact, He took His very best "seed," His Son, Jesus Christ, and He gave that "seed" a specific instruction. Then He buried that "seed" in the earth so He could create a new breed of people in the earth, people who were forgiven and born again of the Spirit of God. People who would take on the spiritual nature of the "seed" (Jesus Christ) in the same way that an apple tree takes on the nature of the seed that gave it life!

In the same way that God produced a new "race" of people in the earth by planting a seed for that specific purpose, you can create the miraculous harvest that you are seeking in your life by planting a seed that bears the specific instruction for your miracle. You already have the seed in your hand. In fact, you possess seeds (finances) that have the potential, when rightly invested, to make the rest of your life everything you want it to be. But to make your miracle a reality, you have to plant that seed with the specific instruction of activating God's miraculous power in your life. You have to bury that seed in the ground by giving it to the Lord. You have to let that seed "die" in the soil of God's kingdom so it can give life to your future the same way that Jesus died and was buried so He could give life to all who would come to believe in Him.

David offered his sacrifice for the specific purpose of halting the plague that had taken so many lives. The widow at Zarephath offered her flour and oil to the prophet with the specific instruction of providing her small family with the food they would need to sustain them through the famine. And you need to present your own offering to the Lord for the specific purpose of giving life to the miracle you are seeking from him.

Third, God has already given you the seed that can move you beyond your present situation.

I have sown "seeds" for healing, "seeds" for favor, and "seeds" for financial miracles. I have "planted" financial offerings in the work of God for victory in a struggle, for the benefit of my marriage, and to elicit the favor of God in situations that were beyond my control. And through these many experiences, I have learned that it is impossible to buy God's favor. At the same time, I have learned that a genuine gift of sincere sacrifice can carry a lot of weight with the Lord. A genuine gift can draw attention to one's faith, one's desperation, and one's absolute seriousness about the need at hand.

What is your need? What is the biggest problem you face right now? What miracle do you seek from the hand of God? What dreams consume your thoughts? What goals fascinate your heart? Are you facing a desperate financial situation? Do you lie awake at night trying to find a solution to your problem? Do you feel overwhelmed by your present circumstances? Do you feel alone and without suitable options?

Then let me invite you to sow a seed for the specific purpose of inviting God to get involved in your dilemma. Let me invite you to present a gift to Him that will command His attention and demonstrate your seriousness about the issue that confronts you. Let me encourage you to give an offering to God that will express your heart and highlight your faith and make clear to the Lord your trust in Him.

The gift that He wants you to give is something that is already in your possession. It is already in your hand. You own it and you control it, and it has the potential to give you what you want today or to produce abundance for you tomorrow. But instead, it must be buried in the soil of God's kingdom if you want it to yield a supernatural harvest for you. So like the gift that David gave, your seed must be a costly one. It must be a gift that is truly a sacrifice for you to sow in expectation of your harvest (see 2 Samuel 24:24).

So here's what I want you to do. Before we proceed with the last two chapters of this book, I want you to take three bold steps.

Step 1: I want you to listen to the voice of the Holy Spirit and do exactly what He tells you to do regarding the seed you will sow. This is the amazing thing about the Christian life. You have your own personal relationship with the Holy Spirit and your own direct line of communication with the Lord. You don't need me to tell you what to do. Instead, you can look directly to God for His instructions. I have taught you the biblical principle of sowing a seed for a specific harvest in your life. God will show you exactly what that means for you and exactly how to apply this principle to your present situation. So pray, and listen carefully to the voice of God within your heart. Remember, God always starts the process of leading us by speaking to our hearts.

Step 2: Once you know what kind of a sacrifice God wants you to make, I want you to plant a seed with the expectation of a harvest. Don't just *hope* that your harvest will come; *expect* your harvest to come. Remember, if you do your part, God is bound by His own Word to do His part in your life. Do your part by planting your seed in the kingdom of God, and then expect the Lord to respond to you in a practical and measurable way.

Step 3: As you plant your seed, I want you to give that seed an "assignment." As you offer your gift to the Lord, I want you to tell Him exactly why you are making your sacrifice. Tell Him that you have a problem that requires His help. Tell Him that you believe in Him and that you trust Him. Tell Him that you have confidence in His wisdom and His ability to solve your problem and meet your need. And tell Him that you are sowing this particular seed so He will respond to your act of faith and intervene in your situation. Remember, a seed of nothing will produce a season of nothing. Nothing leaves heaven until something leaves earth.

Whatever you place in God's hand is destined to multiply. For example, when the widow at Zarephath used the last of her flour and oil to make a small loaf of bread for the prophet, God made sure her barrel of flour and her cruse of oil remained full for as long as the famine endured. When the little boy placed his five small loaves of bread and two fish in the hands of Jesus, five thousand people ate until they were filled, and the disciples collected enough leftovers to feed many more people. And when God sacrificed His one and only Son on the cross and allowed His Son to be buried in the ground, He brought "many sons to glory" (Hebrews 2:10).

The lesson, therefore, is that your seed produces more of itself and it reproduces itself proportionately. So what you give is what you get. If you give fish and bread, you will get fish and bread in return. If you give flour and oil, you will get flour and oil in return. And if you give your one and only Son, you will get a family of sons and daughters in return for your investment. But you get your fish and bread proportionately, and you get your flour and oil proportionately.

If you sow a small gift in the kingdom of God, that gift will definitely multiply, but it will multiply proportionately, and you will reap a small harvest. If you sow a larger gift, however, that seed will multiply proportionately, as well, and you will reap a much larger harvest as a result of your larger sacrifice. In fact, if you put nothing in God's hands at all, even your "nothing" will multiply proportionately: Nothing times nothing is nothing.

Learn to give to the Lord. And while you ought to tithe as an act of obedience and worship, you should learn to give special gifts beyond your tithe that are attached to specific needs and specific prayer requests. But don't give to God in an effort to bribe Him or to pay Him off. We're not talking about blackmail here, and God isn't offering you "protection." He's your Father, not your godfather. When you give to the Lord, therefore, your attitude will be just as important to Him as your gift. The motivation behind your gift will make your gift valuable or worthless in the Lord's eyes, because it's all about trust. It's all about respect. It's all about priorities. It's all about showing God in a real, tangible way that he is more important to you than you are to yourself, and He is a much higher priority in your life than the material wealth that your "seed" could produce for you in the future. And your gift will show that you trust Him, even when your circumstances look bleak.

Show God that you mean business. Show Him that you understand that your present situation can't work out for you unless He gets personally involved. God responds to the desperate cries of His people. The person who is desperate for God's power and desperate for God's goodness is the person who will take desperate measures to show that His need and His faith are more than passing interests; they are very real. And God will respond to such measures in a very real way.

The person who would take something that is valuable and "plant" that thing in the kingdom of God as an offering to the Lord is a person who is first of all desperate. But he also is a person who has tremendous faith in God and a tremendous ability to trust the Lord to do what He said He would do. He is a person who fully anticipates a harvest from His humble "seed." And God is moved by this kind of devotion. He is stirred by this kind of passion. You can count on the fact, therefore, that He will never disappoint the person who approaches Him with this kind of fervency and faith.

CHAPTER 7

Trust the Lord

**When you can't see God's hand,
trust in his plan for your life.**

Have you ever driven through Rhode Island? Rhode Island is a beautiful place. But if you live in another part of the country, one of the first things you notice about Rhode Island is the small size of the state. In fact, Rhode Island is the smallest of the fifty states, even smaller than Hawaii. It is about 48 miles long (north to south) and about 37 miles wide (east to west). That means that the entire state of Rhode Island is only about twice the size of the city of Jacksonville, Florida.

It is difficult to drive through the state of Rhode Island in either direction without traveling through Providence, the state capital and the largest city in Rhode Island. Providence was founded in 1636 by Roger Williams, a religious exile from the Massachusetts Bay Colony, and the city was named by Williams in honor of "God's merciful providence." I mention the capital of Rhode Island here, because every time I hear the name *Providence*, it reminds me of the same merciful providence of God that seemingly directed the life of Roger Williams.

Divine providence is a subject that is rarely mentioned these days in America's pulpits. In past generations, preachers seemed to put a lot more emphasis on providence than they do today. But I am still convinced that providence is one of the most important aspects of God's work in the believer's life.

Providence is simply "the protective care of God." Providence may also be defined as "God's timely preparation for future eventualities." Sometimes we forget about providence, but, without it, life would indeed be a fearful and frightening venture. With divine providence we have the assurance that our lives have direction and purpose, and we have the assurance that God is the ultimate controlling force in the important matters of our lives. Without providence there are no guarantees in life and there are no guiding principles upon which we can rely. Life is little more than a shot in the dark. It is a game of risk and of chance in a universe that is governed by nothing more than mathematical probabilities.

People just cannot live under the fearful belief that life has no purpose, no direction, no guarantees, and no guiding hand that is determining its outcome. For this reason, those who reject the Gospel are forced to find some other "power" upon which they can rely and upon which they can base their lives. From the dawn of human history, people have turned to manmade gods to provide them with an explanation for life (idolatry). They have fabricated their own deities to explain the cataclysmic events of nature (mythology). They have assigned divine power to inanimate objects (animism). They have looked to the sun, moon, and stars for guidance (astrology). And in more recent years, they have looked to the collective abilities of a unified human race as the remedy to all their concerns (humanism) and to human government as the source for all their needs (socialism).

But, for the believer, the most basic teaching of the Bible is that God created the universe and every human being living within the universe. And because of God's existence, every life has a purpose and every person has a destiny. Christians also hold to the belief that God alone determines the purpose of things and the destiny of each individual and that, when necessary, He personally intervenes in the lives of individuals to cause their destinies to unfold. This is divine providence, the belief that God is in control of the universe and in control of everything that happens within the universe. He made all things, and He is the ultimate controlling force behind all things. Nothing happens without His knowledge and consent, and He acts at will to carry out His purposes in human history and in the lives of those who serve Him.

I believe in providence. According to the Bible, God controls the inanimate elements of creation (see Job 38:32; Psalm 135:6–7), He controls the animals (see Matthew 6:26, 10:29), He controls seemingly "random" or "chance" events (see Proverbs 16:33), He controls the affairs of nations (see Job 12:23; Daniel 4:34–35), and He controls all the aspects of our individual lives (see Job 14:5; Psalm 139:16; Proverbs 20:24). God is truly the architect of life, the mastermind behind all that occurs, and the One who manages the control booth of the universe.

So here's the point that I want to make. In fact, here are the two points I want to make about God and His providence in our lives. First, we should never forget that most of God's work is the work He does behind the scenes, out of sight and out of mind. Second, we need to learn to trust what He is doing.

These two thoughts, which are based on the biblical concept of providence, are vitally important for the individual who is seeking a miracle from the hand of God. Over and over, the Bible teaches us that we are incapable of understanding God. It teaches us that "my thoughts are not your thoughts, neither are your ways my ways,' declares the LORD. 'As the heavens are higher than the earth, so are my ways higher than your ways and my thoughts than your thoughts'" (Isaiah 55:8–9). In the Bible we are asked, "Who has known the mind of the Lord so as to instruct him?" (1 Corinthians 2:16). And we are questioned, "Who has known the mind of the Lord? Or who has been his counselor?" (Romans 11:34).

The writers of Scripture have relentlessly put forth the eternal truth that God is God, and that we are not God. We are not all-knowing like Him. We are not all-seeing like Him. We are not able to live in the past, present, and future simultaneously like He is capable of doing. Even though He is our heavenly Father and we are His adored children, there is an infinite gulf between humanity and deity that we must never underestimate.

Our God is an awesome God who is far more glorious and far more powerful than we have the capacity to comprehend. He is limitless in all His ways; therefore, we are incapable of seeing Him at work in our lives. He does what He does behind the scenes and out of sight. He does what He does in His own way and in His own time and without appearing before the bar of our reason to explain Himself to us. Yet He never fails to accomplish His purposes in our lives, and He never fails to honor His promises.

Just ask any seasoned saint about the faithfulness of God and watch tears well up in that person's eyes. Did this experienced believer have challenges along the way? Absolutely! Did this tested Christian have times when he wasn't able to see God's hand at work in his life? Of course! Did this weathered veteran of the army of God doubt the Lord on occasion? You betcha!

But over the years, this believer has come to realize that God has never been far from him and that God has always been working in his life. Sometimes God works silently behind the scenes, and sometimes He works openly in plain sight. But even when we aren't able to see His hand, we can always trust His heart because He never fails to keep His promises or to achieve His purposes in our lives. And nobody knows this better than those seasoned men and women who have walked with the Lord through many circumstances over many years of time.

This kind of life experience builds faith—the rich, deep, enduring kind of faith that leads to trust. And, in the end, that's what faith is really all about: It is trust. Nothing more! Nothing less! We must eventually come to the place where we genuinely trust the Lord.

I have learned so many lessons about my own relationship with God by looking at my relationship with my son, Solomon. Several years ago, when my wife, Christine, and I were driving home one night after a lengthy trip to another state, Solomon was asleep in the backseat of the car. It was late, and, as many young children tend to do, Solomon woke up and stuck his head into the front seat, and asked, "Dad, are we there yet?"

"No, we're not there yet," I told him. "We'll be there soon."

Then he asked me a very interesting question for a five-year old. He said, "Where are we?"

I gave him the highway coordinates and the name of the nearest town, knowing that these interesting facts would have absolutely no meaning to him. Then Solomon simply replied, "Oh!" And he crawled back onto his warm spot on the back seat and returned to the land of slumber. The next morning he woke up in his own bed, wearing his pajamas. And he never gave a thought to how he got there.

Some time later, I started thinking about this event and this little exchange with my son. I realized that Solomon was relating to me the same way that we adults often relate to God. When we feel a little uncertain about things, we demand an accounting from the Lord. We demand all the facts and all the geographical coordinates (as if that information is going to be meaningful to us). Then, with no other recourse before us, we simply go about our daily routines and go to bed at night like we have done ten thousand times before. And somehow, some way, we wake up the next morning in our own beds, and we never give any thought to how God managed to get us home and get us into our pajamas. We just take His abilities for granted.

I was actually deeply moved by the fact that my five-year-old son could return to his seat and go back to sleep when I had given him such an incomplete answer to his question. This showed me that he trusted me completely. And the fact that he never mentioned the episode the following morning is a further indication that Solomon has completely accepted my ability to take care of him and to get him safely home, no matter where we might roam as a family.

This is what God wants from me and from you. He wants our trust. He wants us to be able to curl up in the back seat and let Him drive the car. I'm sure He is amused by our occasional expressions of concern and our occasional barrage of questions. But in the end, He will get us home. He will deal with all the traffic, find the necessary fuel, drive late into the night, if necessary, and then carry us in His arms into our own bedrooms and slip our pajamas on us as He tucks us into bed. And when the morning light dawns, we won't even be aware of all that He did while we were sleeping. All we will need to know is that He took care of us. He knows what He is doing, and we can trust Him without hesitation.

The doctrine of divine providence tells me that God is in control of my life. He is in control of everything. So I can trust Him, and I don't need to worry or to "sweat" the details of my future. The doctrine of divine providence also tells me that God does most of His work when I am not looking. He fulfills His purposes and keeps His promises usually without showing His hand. Methodically, systematically, and in His own time and His own way, He does what He has promised He will do.

So God's actions, which are usually performed behind the scenes, have a way of sneaking up on us. In fact, they sneak up on us in a couple of ways. First, they sneak up on us because we don't see them coming until the last piece of the puzzle finally falls into place. Second, they sneak up on us because we get busy with our lives and we forget that God has been hearing our prayers all along and that He has been busy answering those prayers behind the scenes.

In the same way that my son returned to his nap in the back seat of the car, you and I will typically pray about something and then return to all the demanding circumstances of life that require our time and our attention, and we will forget that God is working to answer our prayers. But even though we may forget about our problems, God never forgets about them. If He has made a promise to us, He will keep that promise no matter how long it takes.

I think it goes without saying that God's timetable isn't the same as yours and mine. Obviously, we want relief from our pains right now. Today! We don't want to wait to be healed, delivered, or blessed. We have needs, and nothing is more important to us at any given moment than a resolution to those needs. So if God really cares for us, He should join us in making our needs His highest priority.

God, however, sees a bigger picture, and He is more interested in our spiritual wellbeing than our temporary comfort. He will rarely do things the way that we want Him to do them or according to the timetable that you and I demand of Him. God is never in a hurry, because time is irrelevant to Him. But He is interested in making us the people He created us to be. So while we are anxious to have our needs met and our problems solved, God is interested in strengthening our faith and developing our character. Consequently, everything He chooses to do or not to do in our lives will be determined by His broader perspective on life and eternity.

I say all this, not because I want to deplete your faith. I have used a lot of ink in the preceding pages to build your faith and to help you appreciate God's willingness and ability to perform miracles. But I tell you all this to make you aware of God's providence in your life and to help you apply an understanding of God's providence to your present situation. When I look back over my own life, I can see God's hand every step of the way, from the time I was born until this present day. In fact, I cannot think of a time or a situation or a challenging circumstance in my life when God was not there to help me. I may not have been able to recognize His involvement at the time, but in hindsight I can see that He was always there and He was always working on my behalf behind closed doors.

So when it comes to the miracle that you need from the Lord, I want you to understand that divine providence is at work in your life, too. But in the same way that you could not fully see or perceive God's involvement in your past until His purposes were finally achieved in your life, you will be unable to see or perceive God's involvement in your present circumstances until all those circumstances are resolved and you have the benefit of 20/20 hindsight to help you better grasp what God has been doing for you.

When you accepted Jesus Christ as your Savior and placed your life in His hands, He took your decision very seriously. God took your step of faith seriously because He regards your life as a precious treasure that He holds close to His heart. He regards your soul as a sacred trust that you have placed under His care. And He regards your problems as His own, because He is your Savior in every sense of that word. But in the same way that a parent performs most of his loving acts for his child without the child's knowledge or understanding, God operates in the secret and private places of divine providence to accomplish His eternal purposes in your life. And He will not relent or withdraw until all His purposes for you have been fulfilled in heaven and in earth. You can count on Him! You can trust Him!

If it seems like your miracle is being delayed, if it seems like God has disappeared and He isn't responding to your cries for help, just keep doing what you are doing. Keep praying, keep believing, keep doing your part to make the miracle a reality, keep planting your seeds of obedience and worship, and keep sleeping in the back seat of the car. God will get you home. Somehow, some way, He will do the right thing at the right time to manifest His glory and His power, as well as His love for you.

There's a little word that I keep seeing a lot in the New Testament, and this little word is really beginning to make an impression on me. Especially in the book of Acts, this word keeps popping up all the time. It's the little word *suddenly*. Whenever this word appears, God's people are usually minding their own business and faithfully performing the routine tasks of their lives; then *suddenly*, God shows up to do something they never saw coming, something that truly catches them off guard because they are preoccupied with life's ordinary demands.

Acts 1:10 – They were looking intently up into the sky as he was going, when *suddenly* two men dressed in white stood beside them.

Acts 2:2 – *Suddenly* a sound like the blowing of a violent wind came from heaven and filled the whole house where they were sitting.

Acts 8:39 – When they came up out of the water, the Spirit of the Lord *suddenly* took Philip away, and the eunuch did not see him again, but went on his way rejoicing.

Acts 9:3 – As he neared Damascus on his journey, *suddenly* a light from heaven flashed around him.

Acts 10:30 – Cornelius answered: "Three days ago I was in my house praying at this hour, at three in the afternoon. *Suddenly* a man in shining clothes stood before me."

Acts 12:7 – *Suddenly* an angel of the Lord appeared and a light shone in the cell. He struck Peter on the side and woke him up. "Quick, get up!" he said, and the chains fell off Peter's wrists.

Acts 16:26 – *Suddenly* there was such a violent earthquake that the foundations of the prison were shaken. *At once* all the prison doors flew open, and everyone's chains came loose.

There are some common threads that connect all these events. In almost every one of these situations, for example, someone was praying. In almost every one of these situations, someone was facing desperate or challenging circumstances that required divine intervention from above. And in almost every one of these situations, nobody could see the hand of God until God finally chose to show His hand. Yet God was working all along behind the scenes to respond to the needs of His people at just the right moment and in just the right way. He was working to effect a physical answer to the spiritual prayers of His people so their faith could produce some tangible results in the physical world where they dwelled.

Perhaps nobody understood this principle of divine providence better than King David. David faced a lot of urgent situations in his lifetime that required the direct intervention of God. In fact, if God had not intervened in David's life from time to time, David would not have survived to fulfill his destiny in the plan of God. But God intervened for David when David faced Goliath with a slingshot and five smooth stones. God intervened for David when David was on the run from King Saul and later from his own son, Absalom. If God had not come through for David, evil would have prevailed and the vision that God had given to David for his life would have been snuffed out. David himself would have died prematurely.

But God never failed to come through for David, not always as quickly as David would have liked, but always with faithfulness. Not always according to David's timetable, but always in the nick of time! Perhaps this is why David, when he grew older, could say, "Rest in the LORD, and wait patiently for him" (Psalm 37:7, KJV).

David knew the value of patience. He knew the rewards of faithful waiting during those long periods of apparent inactivity by

God on his behalf. Over the course of many years and after walking through many dark and dangerous valleys, David finally learned that God is frequently silent, but God is never far away. He is often unobservable, but He is never detached. He is always working behind the scenes to accomplish His purposes in our lives and to fulfill His promises to us. And, in the right time and the right way, He will "suddenly" show His hand. He will "suddenly" burst through the fog and reveal to us what He has been doing for us in the secret chambers of Heaven. He will let us know in a big way that He has always been there and He has always been working on our behalf.

So don't give up, and don't lose heart. Hang in there. The world will test your faith by tempting you to believe that God doesn't care about you or that He doesn't even exist. The people of the world may even mock you or encourage you to rebel against the Lord (see Job 2:9). Your own flesh will test your faith by tempting you to become impatient or by tempting you to show self-pity when things aren't going your way or moving fast enough for your liking. And the devil will test your faith by tempting you to abandon the purposeful pursuit of your miracle and to adopt another plan for your life and your future.

But if you will "rest in the LORD, and wait patiently for him," constantly reminding yourself that God sits in the control booth of the universe and in the control booth of your life, the Lord will, in His time and His way, suddenly burst upon the scene to honor your faith and to vindicate your trust in Him. He will not abandon you. He will not fail you. He will not turn His back on you.

After Noah and his small family had floated in a dark, windowless boat on the floodwaters of the deep for 150 days without hearing a single word from God, "God remembered Noah" (Genesis 8:1). And God will remember you, too. Never forget that He is busy right now, working on your behalf in the same way He was working behind the scenes in Noah's life to fulfill his eternal purposes in the world. You may not be able to see God every time you need visual confirmation of His love and you may not be able to hear Him every time you feel like you need an update on the highway coordinates of your journey. But divine providence will compel the Lord to finish what He has started in your life and what He has promised to do for you. Your job is to remain faithful. Your job is to keep doing what God has given you to do. God's job is to look at the bigger picture and to do the right thing for your eternal wellbeing. But rest assured! In the right time and in the right way, God's providence will come shining through for you in a sudden and unforgettable way.

CHAPTER 8

Prepare for Your Miracle

**As you wait for the manifestation
of your miracle, learn to respect the tension
that exists between "now" and "not yet."**

When we hear the word *tension*, we tend to have negative
thoughts in our minds and negative feelings in our hearts. To
most of us, tension is not a good thing; it is a bad thing.

But tension isn't always bad. Obviously, there is a negative kind
of tension that results in conflict and division. But there also are
healthy forms of tension spread throughout the universe, and I
believe these healthy types of tension are designed to maintain life
and to keep everything in its proper balance.

For example, take a long, hard look at the moon this evening as it
glows in the nighttime sky. As you stare at the moon, think about the
forces that keep the moon in its place. Since the day God created the
moon, something has held that massive heavenly body in suspension
exactly 238,900 miles from Earth. If the moon should wander just a
few miles farther from Earth, it would slip out of its orbit and hurl

into the infinite recesses of space. If the moon should wiggle just a few miles closer to Earth, Earth's gravitational pull would cause the moon to collide with our home planet, and life as we know it would cease.

But the moon just hangs there, seemingly motionless, and it hasn't wandered an inch out of its assigned position since the day God formed it and placed it in the sky. And it hangs there because of tension, the tension that exists between gravity and centrifugal force. Gravity pulls the moon toward the Earth, keeping it from flying into outer space. But the centrifugal force that results from the moon's geocentric orbit around Earth pulls the moon away from Earth with an energy that equals the opposing gravitation force. As a result, the tension that exists between the gravitational pull of Earth and the centrifugal force of the moon's orbit works to keep the moon stationary in its relationship to Earth.

God also has placed a useful tension in the human family to keep the family balanced and healthy. When God created woman, for instance, He designed a creature that is in many ways the exact opposite of man. A woman's physical features are exactly opposite of those of a man so that man and woman can come together to conceive children. But the emotional and psychological composition of man and woman are opposite in many ways, as well, for a very good reason.

For the vast majority of men, the greatest psychological need in their lives is the need for challenges and victories. But for the vast majority of women, the greatest psychological need is the need for security and intimacy. So even though the demarcations between men and women aren't always consistent or predictable, for the most part men are fulfilled through their achievements and women are fulfilled through their relationships. Men find their greatest personal satisfaction in the pursuit of their dreams, and women find their greatest personal satisfaction in the relationships they have with the people they love and cherish.

But these two agendas often create tension. While the typical man wants to quit his job and take all the money out of the family's investment portfolio to open that new restaurant he has always dreamed of opening, the typical woman wants to slow down and be more cautious. She is not so willing to release her husband to work 90 hours a week to build a business that might not succeed. And she is not so willing to surrender the security of her financial nest egg to allow her husband to roll the dice on a venture that may not pay off.

The tension that exists between the needs of a man and the needs of a woman are tensions that were designed by God to keep the family healthy and to keep it well adjusted. While one partner may want to forge ahead into the uncharted waters of life, the other partner will usually be more cautious and prudent, forcing a slower excursion into the unknown. And the "tension" will give balance to their decisions.

In addition, the entire premise of political liberty is based on tension. The Constitution of the United States purposely promotes tension between the states and the federal authorities. The Constitution also promotes tension among the three branches of the government itself. And the Bill of Rights guarantees a free press, which means there will always be tension between the government's desire to restrain the free flow of information and the desire of the press to gather that information and disseminate it to the people it serves. So the founding fathers of our country wanted a system that was based on "tension" so that power would always be distributed and our people would always be free.

In fact, if you will open your eyes and look around, you will notice a certain amount of "tension" in almost everything God has made and in most of the enduring institutions of man. And you will notice that this tension is a good thing and a healthy thing, bringing balance to the physical, emotional, and even spiritual aspects of our lives.

In the New Testament, for instance, there were those who wanted to address the congregation every time the church assembled for worship. And even though the apostle Paul refused to discourage this activity, he did try to create balance within the church by asking the others to judge what these people were saying (see 1 Corinthians 14:29). So the tension that Paul created between those who would speak and those who would analyze their words was a tension designed to keep the church healthy and to keep its worship services free from excess. Furthermore, the tension that Paul created between the younger members of the church, who were encouraged to exercise their boldness, and the older members of the church, who were encouraged to exercise their prudence, was also designed to move the church into the future in a way that would not jeopardize its historical roots (see I Timothy 5:1–3; Titus 2:1–8).

We must learn to appreciate tension when that tension is healthy, and we must learn to appreciate the conflicts that healthy tension often creates. Sometimes the necessary tensions of life will be external tensions as the women confront the men or as the listeners confront the public speakers. But at other times, the conflicts will be internal in nature as we wrestle with the contradictions created between the physical demands of life and the spiritual desires of the heart or between the things our hearts are telling us and the opposing rationale of the mind.

This is particularly relevant when it comes to miracles, because the very nature of a miracle requires the believer to find some sort of common ground between the natural world and the spiritual world, between the tangible world and the world of faith. The expectation of a miracle requires the believer to find harmony between two seemingly conflicting realities. While he believes in his heart that the Word of God is true and that the promises God has made to him are reliable, he must also function as a citizen of the natural world while he waits for the promises of God to materialize in his life. He must walk a tightrope of tension between the world that is seen and the world that is unseen.

My advice to you, therefore, is to learn to do what the early believers did. They found a way to wonderfully harmonize their expectations of the future with the current realities of their daily lives. They figured out a way to walk in the Spirit and to live in their own mortal bodies at the same time. And they learned how to do this by appreciating and embracing the "tension" that exists between the kingdom of God and the current realities of this present life.

You see, when Jesus first appeared on the scene, He spoke forcefully and frequently about the kingdom of God. In fact, He repeatedly told His followers that "the kingdom of God is at hand" (Mark 1:15, KJV). And this announcement deeply excited those who pursued Him and believed in Him. In fact, many of these followers left homes and fortunes to devote their lives to the one who would finally make good on those promises of Scripture that pointed to a coming Messiah. And now that the Messiah was here, the world would finally experience the presence of universal righteousness (see Isaiah 11:4–5), mankind would finally live in peace (see Isaiah 2:2–4), the Holy Spirit would finally dominate the affairs of men (see Joel 2:28–30), the new covenant promised by Jeremiah would finally become a reality (see Jeremiah 31:31–34; 32:38–40), sin and sickness would finally be burdens of the past (see Zechariah 13:1; Isaiah 53:5), and the material world itself would feel the joyful benefits of a new age (see Isaiah 11:6–9).

But unfortunately, this never happened. Instead, the one they thought to be the Messiah was crucified and buried, and the light of hope went out for those who trusted in Jesus as the king over this promised kingdom. But then their hopes were revived when Jesus was raised from the dead. Now, for sure, He would "restore the kingdom to Israel" (Acts 1:6). But He didn't. Instead, He ascended into heaven and poured out the promised Holy Spirit upon His few remaining followers.

The members of the early church were rightly confused, and they were faced with a monumental dilemma. On the one hand, Jesus had announced that the kingdom of God was "at hand," and the power of the Holy Spirit in their lives was a clear indication that this was indeed true. On the other hand, many promises regarding the kingdom of God had not yet been realized. There was no universal peace, and the wolf and the lamb were not feeding together (see Isaiah 65:25). So it did not take the members of the church very long to figure out that the kingdom had indeed arrived, but not fully. It was "here," but "not quite." It was "now," but "not yet." And the early Christians learned to walk a fine line between these two realities. They learned to handle the "tension" created by God's promises and the fact that many of those promises still awaited their fulfillment.

The believers learned to accept God's full and free forgiveness, but they also learned to accept the fact that they were not yet perfected and that they needed to grow spiritually (see Philippians 3:7–14). They learned to accept the fact that they were already victorious over death (see 1 Corinthians 3:22), but they also learned to accept the fact that they would still have to die (see Philippians 3:20–22). They learned to walk in the Spirit, but they also learned to live in a sinful world where Satan could willfully attack them (see Galatians 5:16–26). They learned to embrace the truth that they were already justified in the sight of God (see Romans 8:1), but they also learned to embrace the truth that they must face a future judgment (see 2 Corinthians 5:10). So the early believers learned to see themselves as positionally righteous, but not completely righteous in reality. They learned to see themselves as healthy, but not completely free from the presence of sickness or death. They learned to respect the "tension" that exists between the "now" of God's promises and the "not yet" of the full delivery of those promises.

You, too, must learn to live with this healthy tension in your thinking and your life, because the ability to believe God's promises today is absolutely essential if you hope to experience those promises tomorrow. Your ability to truly anticipate your miracle and plan for your miracle right now is essential to receiving that miracle in the days ahead. Because your miracle is not yet fully realized and the manifestation of your miracle is not yet apparent, you must learn to respect the tension that exists between the "now" and the "not yet" of your passionate prayer request.

From my perspective, there are two extremes that you must avoid as you wait for God to answer your prayers and provide you with the miracle you seek. First, you must avoid the tendency that is displayed by most of the people of this world who have no capacity to believe God for anything. Most people claim that they only believe in those things they can see with their own eyes or touch with their own hands. But this approach to life doesn't work.

Even the people who claim that there is no God are forced every day to put their trust in things they cannot see. They are forced to trust the laws of nature. They are forced to trust in the potential of tomorrow. They are forced to trust in the reliability of other people. Whether we like it or not, life in this world necessitates a certain amount of faith in things we cannot see, measure, observe, or quantify.

As you wait for your miracle, therefore, certain people may ridicule you or purposely work to make things harder for you. But these people are actually living hypocritically because they don't live their own lives the way they are suggesting that you should live yours. Avoid their efforts, therefore, to undermine your faith. Avoid their efforts to dilute your confidence in God's power and God's ability.

Second, you must avoid the tendency to live in the make-believe world of presumptive faith. You cannot simply catch hold of an idea with your heart, repeat that thought with your mouth, and then hope for that thing to materialize before your very eyes. Things don't happen in the physical world unless God's natural laws lead to those events *or* God personally injects himself into the situation so He can temporarily suspend one of His physical laws in order to meet your personal needs.

Consequently, you cannot simply "confess" a financial blessing and then go to the bank to cash the check. You cannot jump off a tall building and expect to float gently to the ground because you "confess" a soft landing on your way down. Why? Because if you aren't saying the same thing about your miracle that God is saying, your words of confession will have no weight!

As I have explained throughout this book, God created the laws of His physical universe for a reason, and he honors those fixed laws with the same resolve that He honors the laws of His spiritual kingdom. Most of the time, therefore, God works through natural means to provide our needs and to answer our prayers. He uses other human beings, for instance, to financially bless us (see Luke 6:38). So if you need a miracle, you have to be patient. You have to believe that God has heard your prayer, that the prayer has already been "approved," that the answer is in the pipeline, and that you will see the results in the physical world in God's due time. But until God acts, don't quit your day job. To do so is to presume upon God's miraculous power, and God is not going to yield to the foolishness of presumptive faith.

I know that this balanced approach to faith creates a certain conflict between natural realities and heartfelt belief. That is why I am explaining to you the spiritual concept of "tension" and the necessity for the believer to know that his faith is being honored "now" while the physical manifestation of his faith may "not yet" have appeared. Therefore, learn to live in anticipation. Learn to prepare for your miracle, expect your miracle, and anticipate your miracle even while you continue to function without your miracle's full availability.

There is an interesting story in the Bible that vividly demonstrates how believers are supposed to walk the fine line between the "now" of God's promises and the "not yet" of God's provision. In the book of Nehemiah, we read the account of the rebuilding of the walls of Jerusalem under the leadership of this great man of God.

In 586 B.C., the city of Jerusalem was completely destroyed by the Babylonian army. Most of the citizens of Jerusalem were killed at that time or taken captive. In addition, the temple and royal palace were burned to the ground. And for approximately 50 years, the Jews remained in captivity in Babylonia. Eventually, however, the Babylonian Empire was overthrown, and Cyrus, the king of Persia, allowed some of the Jews to return to their homeland to rebuild their temple. Nearly a century after this expedition, however, the walls of Jerusalem remained a pile of rubble.

At that time, Nehemiah, the cupbearer to the king (probably Artaxerxes), requested permission to return to Jerusalem to rebuild the walls of the city. And not only did the king grant Nehemiah's request; he also financed a great deal of the work. Nevertheless, Nehemiah and his followers encountered a lot of opposition from many who were living in Israel at the time. Certain people like Sanballat, Tobiah, and Geshem the Arab ridiculed the work and did everything they could do to oppose it, because they did not want to see the city reemerge and they did not want to see the Jewish nation rise from the ashes.

But when Nehemiah learned about their opposition, he went to the Lord and prayed: "Hear us, O our God, for we are despised. Turn their insults back on their own heads. Give them over as plunder in a land of captivity. Do not cover up their guilt or blot out their sins from your sight, for they have thrown insults in the face of the builders" (Nehemiah 4:4–5). Then like any faithful believer, Nehemiah ignored the taunts of his enemies and moved forward in pursuit of his vision for a fully restored Jerusalem.

Sanballat, Tobiah, and Geshem decided to turn up the heat. They gathered additional allies and sent word to Nehemiah that they intended to attack the city and fight against the workers. Nehemiah took these threats very seriously. In fact, Nehemiah prayed again, asking God to intervene in the situation. But then, Nehemiah did an interesting thing. In Nehemiah 4:9, this great spiritual leader tells us that "we prayed to our God and posted a guard day and night to meet this threat." So while the people prayed and trusted God, they also took precautions to live and survive in the real world until God moved to answer their prayers.

Just think about this for a minute, and try to visualize these events. As the people prayed, Nehemiah developed a plan for defending the city (see Nehemiah 4:13–14). He equipped certain people with swords, spears, and bows. Then He trained these people to use their weapons, and He positioned them strategically at certain weak points around the city that needed to be protected. Finally, He put everybody back to work, rebuilding the walls of Jerusalem. But while one shift of workers labored to construct the walls, another shift was poised to respond to a sudden attack. And "those who carried materials did their work with one hand and held a weapon in the other, and each of the builders wore his sword at his side as he worked" (Nehemiah 4:17–18).

To those with a presumptuous kind of faith, Nehemiah's two-pronged approach to this challenge might seem like a faithless approach. It might seem like Nehemiah lacked the faith he needed to be a truly great leader and that the people lacked faith, as well. Did Nehemiah trust in the Lord's ability to answer his prayers, or didn't he? If he did, why did he find it necessary to take additional precautions to protect the city? Didn't he trust the Lord to meet his needs and to answer his prayers? Didn't he believe in God's ability to save him, to rescue him, and to help him complete the mission the Lord appointed him to fulfill? And didn't the people still believe in the God who had parted the sea when the Jews were fleeing from Egypt?

To all these questions, the answer is, "Yes." Nehemiah did have the faith that was necessary to fulfill his divine calling. He did have the faith that was necessary to achieve his life's purpose. Nehemiah did great things, because his faith was so great. And that is why God devoted an entire book of the Bible to explaining Nehemiah's achievements and the role of Nehemiah in the overall plan of God. Nehemiah was indeed a great man and an example of great faith.

But God recorded these things so that you and I could have a real example from history of how to approach faith in a balanced way. Perhaps better than anyone, Nehemiah understood the tension between the "now" aspect of the supernatural world and the "not yet" aspect of the physical world. While Nehemiah was a man of prayer and a man of faith and while he trusted in God and trusted in God's ability to move heaven and earth on his behalf, Nehemiah also understood that God usually works through natural means to accomplish His purposes. He understood that the answers to our prayers often take time to materialize and they often come through bows and arrows.

Meanwhile (The word *meanwhile* actually appears in Nehemiah 4:10, and the word clearly points to a gap in time between Nehemiah's prayer of faith and the realization of his miracle), the faithful believer must do what is necessary to maintain his life. He must go about the normal requirements of his life and deal with the realities of life that God has placed under his care until God shows up to change those realities. He must be a faithful steward of the things God has given him to do right now in the natural world. Like the servants in Cana, he must busy himself by carrying the water jars and filling them with water. Like the disciples in the countryside, he must keep himself occupied by distributing fish and bread to those people who are hungry. And like Nehemiah, he must do what he has to do to fight against those opponents who would stand between him and the fulfillment of his God-given mission. Then he must trust and wait for God's intervention, whether through natural or supernatural means.

Learn to do your work with one hand while you hold a weapon in the other hand. Learn to pray and trust God while you wield a sword. Learn to appreciate and to embrace the "tension" that exists between your faith and the current realities that confront you as you wait to see the fulfillment of your faith. Learn how to "rest in the LORD, and wait patiently for him" (Psalm 37:7, KJV) while fulfilling your various responsibilities as a husband or a wife, a father or a mother, an employee or a student.

In the same way that you believe that Jesus is coming again to this world, yet you are able to function as a normal human being while you wait for His return, so you must learn to function as a normal human being while you wait for the manifestation of the miracle you have requested from God. At the same time, however, the knowledge that God has heard your prayers and that your miracle is on the way must definitely shape your behavior, your speech, and the decisions you make each day as you go about the responsibilities of your life.

Learn to walk with dignity and character as you navigate the tightrope of "tension" that exists between what is and what will be. Learn to walk in obedience, expecting God to honor his Word, but realizing at the same time that you must be faithful in a faithless world until God shows His hand.

Prepare for your miracle by being a good steward of all that God has given you to do between now and the time that your miracle appears, allowing the Lord to choose the time, the place, and the method for honoring his promise to you. And believe me, if you have genuinely heard from God regarding your miracle and if you are faithful with all that He has placed in your hands to do while you wait for His intervention, He will not let you down. He will show himself more than faithful to you. He will show himself to be a miracle-working God!

CONCLUSION

My Prayer for You

Father, I thank you for all the people who will read this book. I thank you for the faith these people have in You, and I thank You for the desire they have in their hearts to learn more about Your miraculous power. But while I am giving thanks for them, I also want to pray for them, because the person who reads this book is the person who stands in need of a miracle from Your hand. And to that end, I pray that You will show him (or her) Your mighty power.

I pray, Lord, that You will speak to each individual's heart about the specific miracle You want to work in that person's life. I pray that You will show that person through Your Word what you are able to do in the situation that he is facing. As the readers of this book begin to pray for the miracles that they need from heaven, I also ask You to help them take the steps that are necessary to see Your full display of power in their lives. I ask You to help them reduce the influences of doubt that pervade the environments where they live and work, and I ask You to help them start visualizing the results that You have promised to them as they start verbalizing the truths You have shown them about Your abilities.

I also ask You to give them the unbridled faith that can lead them to do what most people would never do: I ask you to give them the faith to wait on You and to invest in You by planting, not only their hopes and dreams, but also their tangible resources in Your kingdom as seed offerings that point to their seriousness. And while the seeds that they plant and the prayers that they pray and the confessions that they make with their mouths "germinate" in the ground and while these precious people patiently wait for the physical manifestation of their spiritual hopes and dreams, I ask You to give them the uncanny ability to go about their lives, functioning joyfully while waiting expectantly for the deliverance that they require.

And when that miracle finally arrives for which they have waited and prayed, I ask You to show them why You have done for them the thing they have requested of You. I ask You to let them see how Your demonstration of power in their lives has advanced Your kingdom and glorified Your name, how it has promoted Your purposes for them and for other people as well. In short, Lord, I ask You to do for them what You have done for me and what You have done for countless others throughout the ages. For the power is Yours and the glory is Yours forever and ever, and You are the God who never disappoints those who trust in You. Amen!

The Miracles of Jesus

In the Introduction to this book and in the first chapter of the book's main text, we learned about God's motivations for performing miracles. God performs miracles to glorify His own name, He performs miracles to strengthen the faith of those who believe in Him and to create faith in the hearts of those who don't, He performs miracles to confirm His Word and to remove barriers to the spread of the Gospel, and He performs miracles to demonstrate His compassion for those in need.

God performs miracles by temporarily setting aside the established laws of His physical creation. He performs miracles by suddenly injecting His hand into situations that would not adequately reflect His will without His personal intervention. So miracles occur when the supernatural interfaces with the natural and when the unseen powers of the spirit world collide with the visible forces of the physical world.

Nowhere is the miraculous more evident than in the life and ministry of Jesus. Jesus performed miracles from the beginnings of His earthly ministry until the moment He ascended into heaven. He also performed miracles for all the same reasons that the Father performed miracles: to bring honor to His name, to create faith in the hearts of men, and to show His compassion for hurting people. And the miracles of Jesus, like all God's miracles in the Bible, were designed to confirm the words He was saying.

Throughout history, the miracles of God have demonstrated the authority of God over all the various aspects of His creation, and the miracles of Jesus did the same for Him. They confirmed His authority over the physical world that He had created and over the spirit world that He had made. They confirmed His authority over sickness and disease. They confirmed His authority over all kinds of infirmities and over death itself.

Below is a list of the miracles of Jesus, categorized according to the facet of God's creation that these various miracles affected. Then following the miracles of Christ, you will find an abbreviated list of some of the more notable miracles performed by the servants of God in the Old and New Testaments.

Miracles permeate the history of God's interactions with man, but the Bible is our only guide regarding the kinds of miracles that God performs. For this reason, you should familiarize yourself with these miracles so you can look to them to help you evaluate the legitimacy of the miracles you seek from the Lord. All Scripture quotations are taken from the New International Version.

AUTHORITY OVER THE PHYSICAL WORLD

Jesus demonstrated His role as creator of the physical universe by manifesting His power over the forces of nature.

Calming the storm

Matthew 8:23–26 (Mark 4:35–39; Luke 8:22–24)

Then (Jesus) got into the boat and his disciples followed him. Suddenly a furious storm came up on the lake, so that the waves swept over the boat. But Jesus was sleeping. The disciples went and woke him, saying, "Lord, save us! We're going to drown!" He replied, "You of little faith, why are you so afraid?" Then he got up and rebuked the winds and the waves, and it was completely calm.

Cursing the fig tree

Matthew 21:18–19

Early in the morning, as Jesus was on his way back to the city, he was hungry. Seeing a fig tree by the road, he went up to it but found nothing on it except leaves. Then he said to it, "May you never bear fruit again!" Immediately the tree withered.

Appearing to his disciples

Luke 24:36–37

While they were still talking about this, Jesus himself stood among them and said to them, "Peace be with you." They were startled and frightened, thinking they saw a ghost.

Initial catch of fish

John 5:4–6

When (Jesus) had finished speaking, he said to Simon, "Put out into deep water, and let down the nets for a catch." Simon answered, "Master, we've worked hard all night and haven't caught anything. But because you say so, I will let down the nets." When he had done so, they caught such a large number of fish that their nets began to break.

Walking on water

John 6:16–19 (Matthew 14:22–26; Mark 6:45–51)

When evening came, his disciples went down to the lake, where they got into a boat and set off across the lake for Capernaum. By now it was dark, and Jesus had not yet joined them. A strong wind was blowing and the waters grew rough. When they had rowed about three or four miles, they saw Jesus approaching the boat, walking on the water.

Second catch of fish

John 21:4–6

Early in the morning, Jesus stood on the shore, but the disciples did not realize that it was Jesus. He called out to them, "Friends, haven't you any fish?" "No," they answered. He said, "Throw your net on the right side of the boat and you will find some." When they did, they were unable to haul the net in because of the large number of fish.

Authority over the Spirit World

Jesus demonstrated his role as creator of the spirit world by manifesting his power over the unseen forces of his creation.

Blind and mute demoniac

Matthew 12:22 (Luke 11:14)

Then they brought (Jesus) a demon-possessed man who was blind and mute, and Jesus healed him, so that he could both talk and see.

Afflicted child

Matthew 17: 14–18 (Mark 9:14–27; Luke 9:37–43)

When (Jesus and his disciples) came to the crowd, a man approached Jesus and knelt before him. "Lord, have mercy on my son," he said. "He has seizures and is suffering greatly. He often falls into the fire or into the water. I brought him to your disciples, but they could not heal him." "You unbelieving and perverse generation," Jesus replied, "how long shall I stay with you? How long shall I put up with you? Bring the boy here to me." Jesus rebuked the demon, and it came out of the boy, and he was healed at that moment.

Demoniac in the synagogue

Mark 1:21–26 (Luke 4:31–35)

(Jesus and his disciples) went to Capernaum, and when the Sabbath came, Jesus went into the synagogue and began to teach.... Just then a man in their synagogue who was possessed by an impure spirit cried out, "What do you want with us, Jesus of Nazareth? Have you come to destroy us? I know who you are—the Holy One of God!"

"Be quiet!" said Jesus sternly. "Come out of him!" The impure spirit shook the man violently and came out of him with a shriek.

Daughter of syrophoenician woman

Mark 7:24–30 (Matthew 15:21–28)

Jesus left that place and went to the vicinity of Tyre. He entered a house and did not want anyone to know it; yet he could not keep his presence secret. In fact, as soon as she heard about him, a woman whose little daughter was possessed by an impure spirit came and fell at his feet. The woman was a Greek, born in Syrian Phoenicia. She begged Jesus to drive the demon out of her daughter. "First let the children eat all they want," he told her, "for it is not right to take the children's bread and toss it to the dogs." "Lord," she replied, "even the dogs under the table eat the children's crumbs." Then he told her, "For such a reply, you may go; the demon has left your daughter." She went home and found her child lying on the bed, and the demon gone.

Demoniac of Gadara

Luke 8:26–33 (Matthew 8:28–32; Mark 5:1–13)

(Jesus and his disciples) sailed to the region of the Gerasenes, which is across the lake from Galilee. When Jesus stepped ashore, he was met by a demon-possessed man from the town. . . . When he saw Jesus, he cried out and fell at his feet, shouting at the top of his voice. . . . Jesus asked him, "What is your name?" "Legion," he replied, because many demons had gone into him. And they begged Jesus repeatedly not to order them to go into the Abyss. A large herd of pigs was feeding there on the hillside. The demons begged Jesus to let them go into the pigs, and he gave them permission. When the demons came out of the man, they went into the pigs, and the herd rushed down the steep bank into the lake and was drowned.

AUTHORITY OVER SICKNESS, DISEASE, AND PHYSICAL DEFORMITY

Jesus was best known for his ability to heal those who were suffering from some type of physical malady.

Cleansing the leper

Matthew 8:1–3 (Mark 1:40–42; Luke 5:12–13)

When Jesus came down from the mountainside, large crowds followed him. A man with leprosy came and knelt before him and said, "Lord, if you are willing, you can make me clean." Jesus reached out his hand and touched the man. "I am willing," he said. "Be clean! Immediately he was cleansed of his leprosy.

Centurion's servant

Matthew 8:5–13 (Luke 7:1–10)

When Jesus had entered Capernaum, a centurion came to him, asking for help. "Lord," he said, "my servant lies at home paralyzed, suffering terribly." Jesus said to him, "Shall I come and heal him?" The centurion replied, "Lord, I do not deserve to have you come under my roof. But just say the word, and my servant will be healed. For I myself am a man under authority, with soldiers under me. I tell this one, 'Go,' and he goes; and that one, 'Come,' and he comes. I say to my servant, 'Do this,' and he does it." When Jesus heard this, he was amazed and said to those following him, "Truly I tell you, I have not found anyone in Israel with such great faith. I say to you that many will come from the east and the west, and will take their places at the feast with Abraham, Isaac and Jacob in the kingdom of heaven. But the subjects of the kingdom will be thrown outside, into the darkness, where there will be weeping and gnashing of teeth." Then Jesus said to the centurion, "Go! Let it be done just as you believed it would." And his servant was healed at that moment.

Woman with the flow of blood

Matthew 9:20–22 (Mark 5:21–34; Luke 8:40–48)

Just then a woman who had been subject to bleeding for twelve years came up behind him and touched the edge of his cloak. She said to herself, "If I only touch his cloak, I will be healed." Jesus turned and saw her. "Take heart, daughter," he said, "your faith has healed you." And the woman was healed at that moment.

Two blind men

Matthew 9:27–30

As Jesus went on from there, two blind men followed him, calling out, "Have mercy on us, Son of David!" When he had gone indoors, the blind men came to him, and he asked them, "Do you believe that I am able to do this?" "Yes, Lord," they replied. Then he touched their eyes and said, "According to your faith let it be done to you"; and their sight was restored.

Peter's mother-in-law

Mark 1:29–31 (Matthew 8:14–15; Luke 4:38–39)

As soon as they left the synagogue, they went with James and John to the home of Simon and Andrew. Simon's mother-in-law was in bed with a fever, and they immediately told Jesus about her. So he went to her, took her hand and helped her up. The fever left her and she began to wait on them.

Deaf and dumb man

Mark 7:31–35

Then Jesus left the vicinity of Tyre and went through Sidon, down to the Sea of Galilee and into the region of the Decapolis. There some people brought to him a man who was deaf and could hardly talk, and they begged Jesus to place his hand on him. After he took him aside, away from the crowd, Jesus put his fingers into the man's ears. Then he spit and touched the man's tongue. He looked up to heaven and with a deep sigh said to him, "*Ephphatha!*" (which means "Be opened!"). At this, the man's ears were opened, his tongue was loosened and he began to speak plainly.

Blind man in Bethsaida

Mark 8:22–25

They came to Bethsaida, and some people brought a blind man and begged Jesus to touch him. He took the blind man by the hand and led him outside the village. When he had spit on the man's eyes and put his hands on him, Jesus asked, "Do you see anything?" He looked up and said, "I see people; they look like trees walking around." Once more Jesus put his hands on the man's eyes. Then his eyes were opened, his sight was restored, and he saw everything clearly.

Paralytic in Capernaum

Luke 5:17–26 (Matthew 9:1–7; Mark 2:1–12)

One day Jesus was teaching, and Pharisees and teachers of the law were sitting there. They had come from every village of Galilee and from Judea and Jerusalem. And the power of the Lord was with Jesus to heal the sick. Some men came carrying a paralyzed man on a mat and tried to take him into the house to lay him before Jesus. When they could not find a way to do this because of the crowd, they went up on the roof and lowered him on his mat through the tiles into the middle of the crowd, right in front of Jesus. When Jesus saw their faith, he said, "Friend, your sins are forgiven." The Pharisees and the teachers of the law began thinking to themselves, "Who is this fellow who speaks blasphemy? Who can forgive sins but God alone?" Jesus knew what they were thinking and asked, "Why are you thinking these things in your hearts? Which is easier: to say, 'Your sins are forgiven,' or to say, 'Get up and walk'? But I want you to know that the Son of Man has authority on earth to forgive sins." So he said to the paralyzed man, "I tell you, get up, take your mat and go home." Immediately he stood up in front of them, took what he had been lying on and went home praising God. Everyone was amazed and gave praise to God.

Man with shriveled hand

Luke 6:6–10 (Matthew 12:9–13; Mark 3:1–5)

One another Sabbath (Jesus) went into the synagogue and was teaching, and a man was there whose right hand was shriveled. The Pharisees and the teachers of the law were looking for a reason to accuse Jesus, so they watched him closely to see if he would heal on the Sabbath. But Jesus knew what they were thinking and said to the man with the shriveled hand, "Get up and stand in front of everyone." So he got up and stood there. Then Jesus said to them, "I ask you, which is lawful on the Sabbath: to do good or to do evil, to save life or to destroy it?" He looked around at them all, and then said to the man, "Stretch out your hand." He did so, and his hand was completely restored.

Woman with spirit of infirmity

Luke 13:10–13

On the Sabbath Jesus was teaching in one of the synagogues, and a woman was there who had been crippled by a spirit for eighteen years. She was bent over and could not straighten up at all. When Jesus saw her, he called her forward and said to her, "Woman, you are set free from your infirmity." Then he put his hands on her, and immediately she straightened up and praised God.

Man with dropsy

Luke 14:1–4

One Sabbath, when Jesus went to eat in the house of a prominent Pharisee, he was being carefully watched. There in front of him was a man suffering from abnormal swelling of his body. Jesus asked the Pharisees and experts in the law, "Is it lawful to heal on the Sabbath or not?" But they remained silent. So taking hold of the man, he healed him and sent him on his way.

Ten lepers

Luke 17:11–14

Now on his way to Jerusalem, Jesus traveled along the border between Samaria and Galilee. As he was going into a village, ten men who had leprosy met him. They stood at a distance and called out in a loud voice, "Jesus, Master, have pity on us!" When he saw them, he said, "Go, show yourselves to the priests." And as they went, they were cleansed.

Servant of the high priest

Luke 22:47–51

While (Jesus) was still speaking a crowd came up, and the man who was called Judas, one of the Twelve, was leading them. He approached Jesus to kiss him, but Jesus asked him, "Judas, are you betraying the Son of Man with a kiss?" When Jesus' followers saw what was going to happen, they said, "Lord, should we strike with our swords?" And one of them struck the servant of the high priest, cutting off his right ear. But Jesus answered, "No more of this!" And he touched the man's ear and healed him.

Nobleman's son

John 4:46–51

Once more (Jesus) visited Cana in Galilee, where he had turned the water into wine. And there was a certain royal official whose son lay sick at Capernaum. When this man heard that Jesus had arrived in Galilee from Judea, he went to him and begged him to come and heal his son, who was close to death. "Unless you people see signs and wonders," Jesus told him, "you will never believe." The royal official said, "Sir, come down before my child dies." "Go," Jesus replied, "your son will live." The man took Jesus at his word and departed. While he was still on the way, his servants met him with the news that his boy was living.

Invalid at Pool of Bethesda

John 5:2–9

Now there is in Jerusalem near the Sheep Gate a pool, which in Aramaic is called Bethesda and which is surrounded by five covered colonnades. Here a great number of disabled people used to lie— the blind, the lame, the paralyzed. One who was there had been an invalid for thirty-eight years. When Jesus saw him lying there and learned that he had been in this condition for a long time, he asked him, "Do you want to get well?" "Sir," the invalid replied, "I have no one to help me into the pool when the water is stirred. While I am trying to get in, someone else goes down ahead of me." Then Jesus said to him, "Get up! Pick up your mat and walk." At once the man was cured; he picked up his mat and walked.

Blind man at Pool of Siloam

John 9:1–7

As he went along, (Jesus) saw a man blind from birth. His disciples asked him, "Rabbi, who sinned, this man or his parents, that he was born blind?" "Neither this man nor his parents sinned," said Jesus, "but this happened so that the works of God might be displayed in him…. After saying this, he spit on the ground, made some mud with the saliva, and put in on the man's eyes. "Go," he told him, "wash in the Pool of Siloam" (this word means "Sent"). So the man went and washed, and came home seeing.

AUTHORITY OVER DEATH

The Bible describes death as "the last enemy" (1 Corinthians 15:26). But Jesus manifested his power even over the seemingly permanent sting of death.

Raising of Jairus' daughter

Matthew 9:18–25 (Mark 5:21–42; Luke 8:40–55)

While (Jesus) was saying this, a synagogue leader came and knelt before him and said, "My daughter has just died. But come and put your hand on her, and she will live." Jesus got up and went with him, and so did his disciples…. When Jesus entered the synagogue leader's house and saw the noisy crowd and people playing pipes, he said, "Go away. The girl is not dead but asleep." But they laughed at him. After the crowd had been put outside, he went in and took the girl by the hand, and she got up.

Raising the widow's son

Luke 7:11–15

Soon afterward, Jesus went to a town called Nain, and his disciples and a large crowd went along with him. As he approached the town gate, a dead person was being carried out—the only son of his mother, and she was a widow. And a large crowd from the town was with her. When the Lord saw her, his heart went out to her and he said, "Don't cry." Then he went up and touched the bier they were carrying him on, and the bearers stood still. He said, "Young man, I say to you, get up!" the dead man sat up and began to talk, and Jesus gave him back to his mother.

Jesus' own resurrection

Luke 24:1–6 (Matthew 28:1–10; Mark 16:1–7; John 20:1–18)

On the first day of the week, very early in the morning, the women took the spices they had prepared and went to the tomb. They found the stone rolled away from the tomb, but when they entered, they did not find the body of the Lord Jesus. While they were wondering about this, suddenly two men in clothes that gleamed like lightning stood beside them. In their fright the women bowed down with their faces to the ground, but the men said to them, "Why do you look for the living among the dead?" He is not here; he has risen!"

Lazarus raised

John 11:38–44

Jesus, once more deeply moved, came to the tomb. It was a cave with a stone laid across the entrance. "Take away the stone," he said. "But, Lord," said Martha, the sister of the dead man, "by this time there is a bad odor, for he has been there four days." Then Jesus said, "Did I not tell you that if you believe, you will see the glory of God?" So they took away the stone. Then Jesus looked up and said, "Father, I thank you that you have heard me. I knew that you always hear me, but I said this for the benefit of the people standing here, that they may believe that you sent me."

When he had said this, Jesus called in a loud voice, "Lazarus, come out!" The dead man came out, his hands and feet wrapped with strips of linen, and a cloth around his face.

AUTHORITY OVER THE CHALLENGES OF EVERYDAY LIFE

Jesus demonstrated his concern for people and his ability to provide for them in times of need.

Feeding the 4000

Matthew 15:32–38 (Mark 8:1–10)

Jesus called his disciples to him and said, "I have compassion for these people; they have already been with me three days and have nothing to eat. I do not want to send them away hungry, or they may collapse on the way." His disciples answered, "Where could we get enough bread in this remote place to feed such a crowd?" "How many loaves do you have?" Jesus asked. "Seven," they replied, "and a few small fish." He told the crowd to sit down on the ground. Then he took the seven loaves and the fish, and when he had given thanks, he broke them and gave them to the disciples, and they in turn to the people. They all ate and were satisfied. Afterward the disciples picked up seven basketfuls of broken pieces that were left over. The number of those who ate was four thousand men, besides women and children.

The temple tax

Matthew 17:24–27

After Jesus and his disciples arrived in Capernaum, the collectors of the two-drachma temple tax came to Peter and asked, "Doesn't your teacher pay the temple tax?" "Yes, he does," he replied. When Peter came into the house, Jesus was the first to speak. "What do you think, Simon?" he asked. "From whom do the kings of the earth collect duty and taxes—from their own children or from others?" "From others," Peter answered. "Then the children are exempt," Jesus said to him. "But so that we may not cause offense, go to the lake and throw out your line. Take the first fish you catch; open its mouth and you will find a four-drachma coin. Take it and give it to them for my tax and yours."

Feeding the 5000

Luke 9:12–17 (Matthew 14:13–21; Mark 6:30–44; John 6:1–13)

Late in the afternoon the Twelve came to (Jesus) and said, "Send the crowd away so they can go to the surrounding villages and countryside and find food and lodging, because we are in a remote place here." He replied, "You give them something to eat." They answered, "We have only five loaves of bread and two fish—unless we go and buy food for all this crowd." (About five thousand men were there.) But he said to his disciples, "Have them sit down in groups of about fifty each." The disciples did so, and everyone sat down. Taking the five loaves and the two fish and looking up to heaven, he gave thanks and broke them. Then he gave them to the disciples to distribute to the people. They all ate and were satisfied, and the disciples picked up twelve basketfuls of broken pieces that were left over.

Water changed to wine

John 2:1–9

On the third day a wedding took place at Cana in Galilee. Jesus' mother was there, and Jesus and his disciples had also been invited to the wedding. When the wine was gone, Jesus' mother said to him,

"They have no more wine." "Woman, why do you involve me?" Jesus replied. "My hour has not yet come." His mother said to the servants, "Do whatever he tells you." Nearby stood six stone water jars, the kind used by the Jews for ceremonial washing, each holding from twenty to thirty gallons. Jesus said to the servants, "Fill the jars with water"; so they filled them to the brim. Then he told them, "Now draw some out and take it to the master of the banquet." They did so, and the master of the banquet tasted the water that had been turned into wine.

OTHER NOTABLE MIRACLES IN THE BIBLE

Miracles performed through Moses

The ten plagues (Exodus 7–12)

Parting the Red Sea (Exodus 14:21–22)

Water from the rock (Exodus 17:6; Numbers 20:11)

Halting the plague (Numbers 21:8–9)

Miracles performed through Joshua

Parting the Jordan River (Joshua 3:14–17)

The sun and moon stayed (Joshua 10:12–13)

Miracles performed through Elijah

Invoking a drought (1 Kings 17:1)

The meal and oil multiplied (1 Kings 17:13–16)

The child restored to life (1 Kings 17:17–22)

The sacrifice consumed by fire (1 Kings 18:36–38)

Invoking rain to end the drought (1 Kings 18:41–45)

Parting the Jordan River (2 Kings 2:8)

Miracles performed through Elisha

Parting the Jordan River (2 Kings 2:13–14)

The waters healed (2 Kings 2:19–22)

Water supplied (2 Kings 3:9–20)

The widow's oil multiplied (2 Kings 4:1–6)

A child raised to life (2 Kings 4:8–37)

The pottage rendered harmless (2 Kings 4:38–41)

The loaves multiplied (2 Kings 4:42–44)

Naaman healed of leprosy (2 Kings 5:1–14)

Iron caused to float (2 Kings 6:1–7)

A dead man raised to life (2 Kings 13:21)

Miracles performed through Isaiah

The shadow reversed on the stairway (2 Kings 20:1–11; Isaiah 38:1–8)

Miracles performed through Peter

Ananias and Sapphira struck dead (Acts 5:1–10)

Dorcas raised to life (Acts 9:36–41)

Miracles performed through Paul

Elymas blinded (Acts 13:6–12)

Eutychus restored to life (Acts 20:7–12)

Recovery from a venomous snake bite (Acts 28:1–6)

About the Author

Dave Martin, Your Success Coach, is a mentor, inspirational speaker, and business leader with a mission to communicate the Biblical principles of success. Dave is known around the world for his ability to resonate with his audience, providing insights and wisdom that are life changing. Dave shares timeless truths, wrapped in humor and delivered with passion, teaching people how to pursue and possess a life of success.

In addition to speaking regularly in corporations, colleges and churches, Dave is a keynote speaker at Get Motivated events across the nation. He is also a part of the teaching team for Hillsong Church, under the leadership of Brian Houston, and is on the board of Joel Osteen's Champion's Network.

Dave is the author of several best-selling books including *The 12 Traits of the Greats*, *The Force of Favor*, and most recently, *Another Shot*. Thousands have invested in his personal coaching systems and participate in Dave's free weekly development program called *Success Made Simple*.

He is founder and president of Dave Martin International which champions principle-based coaching by connecting, encouraging and investing in business leaders, pastors, entrepreneurs and anyone desiring a life of more. This thriving ministry is based in Orlando, Florida, which is home to Dave, his wife Christine, and their son Solomon.

Follow me.

Keep in touch with live events, timely coaching and ministry in your area!

Twitter   Facebook   Vimeo

@drdavemartin   /davemartininternational   /drdavemartin

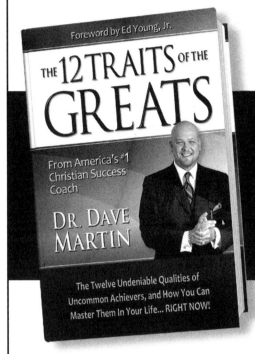

The Harrison House Vision

Proclaiming the truth and the power

Of the Gospel of Jesus Christ

With excellence;

Challenging Christians to

Live victoriously,

Grow spiritually,

Know God intimately.

PRAYER OF SALVATION

God loves you— no matter who you are, no matter what your past. God loves you so much that he gave his one and only begotten Son for you. The Bible tells us that "…whoever believes in him shall not perish but have eternal life" (John 3:16 NIV). Jesus laid down His life and rose again so that we could spend eternity with Him and experience His absolute best on earth. If you would like to receive Jesus into your life, say the following prayer out loud and mean it in your heart.

Heavenly Father, I come to you admitting that I am a sinner. Right now, I choose to turn away from sin, and I ask you to cleanse me of all unrighteousness. I believe that Your son, Jesus, died on the cross to take away my sins. I also believe that he rose again from the dead so that I might be forgiven of my sins and made righteous through faith in him. I call upon the name of Jesus Christ to be the Savior and Lord of my life. Jesus, I choose to follow You and ask You that You fill me with the power of the Holy Spirit. I declare that right now I am a child of God. I am free from sin and full of the righteousness of God. I am saved in Jesus' name. Amen.

If you prayed this prayer to receive Jesus Christ as your Savior for the first time, please contact us to receive a free book by writing to us.

www.harrisonhouse.com
Harrison House
PO Box 35035
Tulsa, Oklahoma 74153

Fast. Easy.
Convenient.

For the latest Harrison House product information and author news, look no further than your computer. All the details on our powerful, life-changing products are just a click away. New releases, email subscriptions, testimonies, monthly specials—find them all in one place. Visit harrisonhouse.com today!

harrisonhouse.com